BONNIE
BODACIOUS

BONNIE BODACIOUS

From the Courtroom to the Cabaret,
an Ecdysiast's Journey

SHANNON VARNER ALEXANDER

BONNIE BODACIOUS, LLC
ATLANTA, GA

Published by Bonnie Bodacious, LLC
bonnie@bonniebodacious.com
bonniebodacious.com

Bonnie Bodacious books are available at special discounts for bulk purchase for sales promotions, premiums, fundraising, and educational needs. Special books or book excerpts also can be created to fit specific needs. For details and permission requests, write to the email address above.

Some names and identifying characteristics have been changed to protect the privacy of the individuals involved.

ISBN 979-8-9885297-0-5 (hardback)
ISBN 979-8-9885297-1-2 (paperback)
ISBN 979-8-9885297-2-9 (eBook)

Printed in the United States of America

—

Book Midwifery by Fen Druadìn
Copyediting by James Gallagher
Cover Design by Jazmin Welch (fleck creative studio)
Author Photo by Stephanie May Saujon of La Photographie
Book Design & Publishing by Kory Kirby
SET IN ADOBE JENSON PRO

I dedicate this book to my mother,
Blythe Faye Ricker.

I am eternally grateful for your generous spirit,
your delight in all living things,
your appreciation of beauty,
and your insistence on carrying my flags into battle
on every front,
no matter whether you understood me or not.

You loved me out loud and with unabashed ferocity,
and that was enough.

CONTENTS

CONTENT WARNING

P ART OF MY JOURNEY AWAY FROM FULLY OCCUPYING my own body stemmed from sexual assaults and rapes I survived during my teens and early twenties. In this book I share those stories in some detail. They are all contained in chapter 5, specifically beginning on page 42 and ending at the bottom of page 47. Please protect your own heart and mind and feel free to skip those pages if you feel that reading about those details might be harmful to you in any way.

THE CONCEPTION & BIRTH OF THIS BOOK

ID THIS BOOK'S TITLE CATCH YOUR EYE? YOUR HEART? Are you in those squeeze years between forty and sixty? Are you wondering if you missed a turn somewhere? Faltering as you juggle your kids or your career—or both—while also caring for older family members who suddenly seem to be as wayward and as irresponsible as teenagers?

I get it. I've lived it. Still am. But I've been lucky enough, or desperate enough, to decide I needed more forks in my road, more paths not taken, and to be one who decided to go wandering in search of something I knew I had lost.

Some of the paths I cut through the wilderness were not unfamiliar. Deciding to move my body and, therefore, to feel it more fully, for example. That's a path I share with many—reconnecting with a long-lost hobby (in my case, scuba diving) and finding joy and fulfillment in something I had previously set aside because it interfered with the responsibilities I rushed to embrace before I knew that cutting off pieces of myself shouldn't be necessary. That's also a path that has shared other feet than mine.

Deciding to modify my body while also learning to love the one I already had, for all its faults, that path has a few more weeds, but I'm not alone there either. The path I pulled my husband toward—social nudity and clothing-optional travel—that path has some brambles along the way and not nearly as many people, but also not as few as you might think.

The path from being a middle-aged woman who shrank away from cameras and bathing suits to being a burlesque performer, at fifty, and being a performance artist who gets as naked as legally allowed on stage while twirling tassels from pasties attached to her areolas with carpet tape, that path is quite a bit quieter. That path took me from passing through the world in the guise of an unassuming straight mom who worked as a lawyer and volunteered with the high school marching band to living out loud and unapologetically as Bonnie Bodacious. That path has been mine alone. It was on *that* path that I tumbled into love with myself, which is not the same as saying I love myself. My tagline, the bit emcees say to announce that I'm taking the stage, sums it up nicely: *Buxom, brazen, bisexual, and bodacious, Bonnie is Atlanta's own burlesque badass!*

As I look back over the last eight years, the years since my mother died way too soon from early-onset dementia, the years since I fully understood the gift she gave me in showing me how time is relentless in its scarcity, the years since I shrugged off convention, reclaimed my body in all its pain and power, and started living fully out loud and without apology, I want nothing more than for other humans to make their own paths into the wilderness, paths that aren't paved or fenced. If my stories can lead others to find the joy, or anything close to it, that the cleaving to my own self has brought me, then I will have no regrets.

WHO & WHY I WAS WHEN MOM GOT SICK

ROM TIME TO TIME I DO AN ACT AS A BURLESQUE performer in which I talk about how I was much older in my twenties than I am now. It's a spoken-word burlesque act where I stand at a microphone and don't so much striptease as defiantly shed layers, all while telling the story of how I found my way back to myself and to my body after devoting my younger adult years to self-recrimination and judgment on a grand scale. At the end I strike a power pose, wearing nothing but rhinestoned shoes, fishnet thigh highs, a flesh-colored merkin rhinestoned to look like a vulva, and a pair of pasties rhinestoned to look like nipples and areolas. It is as naked as I can legally be in most of the venues where burlesque is performed in my town.

It's a powerful act that never fails to connect with the audience.

Conceiving it, performing it, and processing the response of audience members was a significant step toward writing this book. In that act I talk about how my life unraveled when I was in my thirties. In that decade I began an unexpected fitness journey, one I'd never have imagined for myself in a million years. I also was forced to shed expectations of what mattered to me, all while navigating divorce, career crisis, the loss of a home, bankruptcy, coparenting with my former spouse, my mother's devastating early-onset-dementia diagnosis, newly single motherhood, a new love, a job loss, and the blending of my little family (myself and my son) with my new husband's household and his two children.

By the dawn of my forties I thought I was doing mostly OK. I was always exhausted, but that seemed to be a given, I saw my struggles reflected everywhere I looked. After all, I was fully immersed in the squeeze of middle age—parents aging and needing support just when our kids were wrestling with becoming adults in this vicious age of information overwhelm. All while trying to take advantage of my so-called prime earning years.

I'd eventually recovered from being laid off from my big law firm job and had built a small but respectable family law practice as a solo practitioner. I worked hard to balance my time between work and home life and responsibilities, but family law is a practice area that does not lend itself to being left neatly at the office every evening.

My mother and her husband were living in North Carolina, a good six-hour drive from me, at the time she was officially diagnosed with dementia, but there wasn't anyone else to help with her care, to stay engaged with the decisions to be made, and to give my stepfather, Eric, a respite. The glib jokes I'd always made about the joys of being an only child with four parents (divorced, both remarried, all four friendly with each other) bit me in the ass. In addition to juggling my law practice, my household, our kids, and their activities and needs, I was trekking back and forth to Durham every four to six weeks for three to four days at a time. When I wasn't in Durham, I spent lots of time on the phone with my mother, or navigating her care from afar, trying to walk what was frequently a difficult line between cooperation and conflict between myself and Eric over the best solutions.

One of our biggest fears as she rapidly declined mentally and emotionally was that her body would blithely carry her along for another few decades, oblivious to the disintegration playing out inside her skull. Dementia is a terrible way to go, but once she reached the tipping point beyond which catching any glimpse of her old self was gone, it was hard to not want her to be free from the body that trapped her so cruelly. I'd have given anything to have her back, all of her, for all the ways we used to aggravate each other, for all her emotional volatility and drama. I ache to have her back even now. But I will not pretend that it wasn't a gift to her, and to us, when she died on June 8, 2014. While we did have some idea it was coming, that moment still took my breath away. Being with her, breathing in sync with her, wondering if each breath was the last, until, it just . . . *was*, was a gift to both of us. It was a bigger moment than I expected given that it was not a surprise in any sense. The space in the air left by the absence of her next breath rippled through all the aspects of my life like water pierced by a stone. That moment refracted all the light I thought was clear and focused it into a thousand dancing rainbows, just like the prisms she hung from the windows of my bedroom when I was a child.

Since that day, I've rearranged so much of my life, so many of my priorities, that people who knew me then and find me now often don't recognize me. My husband, Dave, and I wrestled with the implication that my own brain may be a ticking time bomb. I have history on both sides of my family, but especially on the maternal side.

Dementia claimed both my mother and her mother. I was forty-two when Mom died. She'd gotten noticeably sick by the time she was fifty-five and steadily thereafter had been limited in her independence and abilities. By her late fifties, she'd been barred from all the things she'd always said she wanted to do someday, though never *today*. All the adventures and travel and shenanigans that might have been—all vanished and scattered like so much shredded paper. As I saw it in that moment after her death, I had thirteen years I could probably count on before things could go awry. I decided to try like hell to do everything I thought I might want to do in this life by the time I turned fifty-five. If I don't get sick (which is possible, as my mother's sister is still going strong at sixty-eight), anything beyond that will be delicious, glorious gravy.

Either way, should I reach those gravy days, I will bathe in the decadence of them without shame. There's certainly nothing wrong with being the old woman in the room with the most interesting stories because she's said yes far more than she's said no. I want to be that woman. And if my brain does short-circuit, well, I've had, and will continue to have, an amazing, full, colorful, and wild ride. I already had some good stories. I'd already lived a few adventures, but there was so much I still wanted to do, and so much I still didn't even know was possible.

I was resigned and not entirely uncomfortable in my middle-aged juggling act. Had my mom lived and stayed whole, she would have supported me in that resignation. It was how she had always lived. She didn't realize the peril of regret until she was past the point of no return. She wasn't able to be vulnerable with me about that until she was too sick to care about crying in my arms. I wish that I could have learned, that she could have learned, the truth about time in a gentler way, but this was the way we learned, together, the thing we always know but easily forget in the day-to-day morass: time is the only thing we cannot make more of.

So here I am, newly fifty, possibly in the decade of my own untimely mental deterioration. And yet I am happy. I am free. I've traveled more than I would have thought "reasonable" before. I've returned to scuba diving, something I'd given up in my early twenties, with a fervency that makes me feel fifteen again. I've had surgery to address challenges I'd resigned myself to for years. I've started dancing again, something I hadn't done for decades. Most shockingly, I discovered that my body, a body I had scorned and abused and all but divorced, was still open and ready for reconciliation with me.

I discovered I could be whole again with the kind of abandon and freedom that came naturally when I first walked this earth. I discovered the joy of being socially nude and of walking on naked tropical beaches. I explored love and recognized and publicly celebrated my sexuality in defiance of expectations for middle-aged women raised in the South. I discovered burlesque, an art form that felt like coming home and waking up all at once. I blossomed into a burlesque performer and was welcomed into a troupe that has become dearer to me than the church I always hoped existed but never quite found. I've worn my hair in a rooster cut for most of the last two years, and I had an asymmetrical side shave for the few years prior to that. It's usually fire-engine red unless I'm changing it up for a show. So many so-called flaws have miraculously become features to celebrate.

I love making people laugh, and cry, and thrum with sensuality. I'm not afraid of the sound of my voice or the shriek of an awkward laugh. I fart and belch with more abandon than my husband would prefer, and then I giggle because human bodies are fucking hilarious *and* glorious, sexy *and* absurd, strong *and* fragile. I no longer apologize in any way for taking up space. I have tumbled deeply into love with myself.

While I have a few more years to go before I hit the Mom-inspired bucket list "deadline" of my fifty-fifth birthday (when I'll hopefully start doing backstrokes in warm, delicious gravy), I am passionately desperate to show others how to find this urgency to live while they still can. To connect people to their bodies again, in all the ways that make their senses sing. Not everyone needs to get physically naked to strip away the trivialities that weigh us down, but physical nakedness was instrumental in my own healing. Whatever judgment you've heaped on yourself, whatever has given you delight from afar but you've denied the call to draw closer, know that it *is* for you. Right now. You are worthy. And falling in love with yourself, deliciously, recklessly even, is your inalienable right. Claim it now. The path will not always be open to you.

BONNIE
BODACIOUS

Chapter One

THE RECKONING: MOM'S DIAGNOSIS & ILLNESS

MY MOTHER, BLYTHE, WAS VIBRANT IN A MUTED WAY. She moved through the world with a bravado cloaked in flowing clothing that hid her form, with antique broaches that announced her quirkiness, with an explosive laugh and a throaty chuckle. She was volatile but frequently suppressed, so much so that when her rage did escape, it startled us all, her most of all, momentarily at least. She had rage that she kept stoked and pulsing, that could leap up and burn in valiant defense of her loved ones, or to fuel her resentment of the very same beloveds. You wanted her on your side in a fight. And you trembled and contorted to avoid attracting her angry gaze when you felt it sweeping the room.

I know I was not alone in this dance with her. My father did it, my stepfather did it, some of her friends even left altogether when the back-and-forth became too exhausting. She was an extrovert whose self-critical views made her act like an introvert. She dulled her fear of rejection and not being enough through alcohol and books—and, later, prescription medication. She had powerful gifts that she feared releasing. Three to four martinis a night, along with an appropriately paired wine for dinner, kept the fear of failure suppressed and her delight in others elevated. Thankfully she was a maudlin drunk rather than a belligerent one. Not that the distinction made it easy to be the child of an alcoholic, but I'm grateful that I don't have too many memories of her yelling or throwing things. She did yell and throw things sometimes, and she had a wicked temper, but more so when sober.

When she drank, she was more inclined to tears, and melancholy, and feeling sorry for herself out loud. Sometimes that meant I felt guilty, sometimes embarrassed, sometimes both. But if I could keep her laughing, she was a delight. She'd come out of her shell and shine with her collectible blown martini glass refracting the light around her face. When she was just the right amount of tipsy, she was at her full strength as the hostess at the head of the table, or curled up on the end of the couch, cackling with laughter as my friends and I cut up and regaled her with tales of the ins and outs of our tortured high school lives.

The absolute best thing about my mother was her ability to fill a dinner table with a variety of misfits and lead them through an evening of conversation, debate, and laughter so that everyone felt utterly at home in her presence. She was never much of a cook, and her marriage to my father was fraught with loneliness due to his shift work and, as I later learned, his infidelity and her shame around it.

They split when I was seven, and after a few years they crafted a working friendship, one in which they both espoused their enduring fondness for the other, from a distance.

My mom was the *parent* in the relationship, but she did everything she could to encourage a healthy bond between me and my father, despite the inconstancy of his schedule (mostly out of his control) and the inconstancy of his affections with other women. Once she was no longer in line to be pierced directly by his behavior, she accepted him as he was and allowed me to love him and get to know him and his faults on my own terms. I am so grateful to her for not following the norms of the seventies and eighties, of doing her best to shield me from her own justifiable anger and hurt around his behavior. But her marriage to my stepfather allowed her to step into the hostess role, one she'd learned well from her own father.

My stepfather was, and is, an introvert. Now, in his later years, he's diagnosed himself as on the autism spectrum, and I believe he has found a great deal of relief in understanding that his oddness is not so terribly odd after all. He is an incredible chef who loves to cook for people in a way that belies his apparent disinterest in them most of the time. Food is language for him, and crafting it and sharing it is the way he connects most readily to other humans. He and my mother were the perfect pair for many years. He did the shopping, he planned the menus, he made the food, and my mother provided a never-ending cast of hungry, grateful people to sit at their table and enjoy it.

I was typically in charge of setting and clearing the table, doing or at least helping with the dishes, and occasionally making a salad. Otherwise I was simply one of their favorite dinner guests. I was a typical only child, a precocious conversationalist, funny, apt to impressions, earnest, and, as a teenager, only occasionally sullen. The shifting cast of interesting misfits who peopled our table night after night drew me out of myself despite my best efforts at sticking to my angsty place in the conversation.

My mother knew everyone, and everyone liked her until or unless they became close enough to upset her. But most people didn't, and I received a whole other level of education around our dinner table. No one spoke to me like a child. I was simply Blythe's daughter. I loved making everyone laugh, but most of all my mom. She and I shared a sense of humor that ran deep, and our eyes would sparkle across the table sometimes, catching the laugh that was coming and holding it, sparkling and incandescent between us, before it exploded across everyone else's consciousness, and then the table would erupt. Even odd, antisocial Eric, my stepfather, would let forth a booming head-tossing laugh before he'd add his own quip, which would set us all off again.

At some point we all noticed things. When she was in her early fifties, they moved out of state to accommodate a job that Eric wanted. I no longer spent time with her almost daily, and we were relegated to frequent phone calls and less frequent visits. Her calls and conversation topics became more repetitive. She wasn't remembering things that were said the day before. She loved their little walkable town and the interesting old house they'd bought with all its old-house problems. She threw herself into overseeing a remodel of the kitchen, and from a distance all seemed basically as it always had been.

Eric's perceptions of any problems may have been dulled by familiarity and hope. Without the social stimulation of others, their dinner table was punctuated more by the rustling of turning pages than by the rumble of conversation. My mom found a few friends in her community, fellow middle-aged dog lovers with whom she could chat over a fence on the way to the coffee shop, but she lost the sense of fundamental belonging that she'd had during a lifetime in Atlanta. There were perks to the move, and my mother came to love her little town and her old creaky house with the gorgeous view of the Ohio River. In hindsight, though, it is clear my mom lost some footing in that move, more than we realized at the time.

For a long while we attributed her incremental increases in forgetfulness and confusion to normal aging and to her alcoholism. We all had moments when we wondered if something darker was happening. But each of us doubled down on keeping that awareness at bay, especially her.

I was deep in law school at this point, treading water, trying to juggle motherhood and grad school, in a marriage that was showing deeper and deeper cracks, while we glibly went further and further into debt. I figured if things got bad enough, Eric would call. And then they moved again, and what little footing Mom had gained after the first move disappeared.

By 2007 my first marriage was on its last legs, and while my husband, Clint, and I knew it, we hadn't told anyone yet. We had just gutted and renovated our home in a last-ditch effort to make each other happy (it didn't work), but we'd made a pact, between him and me, that we were going to host a magnificent family Christmas in our new home, knowing it would actually be both the first in that house and the last for us as an intact family.

All four of my parents (including my recently divorced dad and stepmother) and my aunt descended upon us. All of us were planets orbiting my son, Chase, celebrating him (he was six that year), for what his father and I knew would be his last "normal" pre-divorce Christmas. I did my best, breaking out what could have been an award-winning performance, except for the times I hid in my new walk-in closet, sobbing when I couldn't take the charade for a minute more.

I loved our new kitchen, loved that it was the centerpiece of the house, a command center with views of almost the entire ground floor. I busied myself with cooking and baking, anxious for everything to be picture perfect. Mom's constant questions about what I was doing and why struck me as remarkably childlike. She and Chase seemed to be on similar wavelengths. Some of the more challenging facets of her personality solidified into sharper-than-normal points. Stubbornness bordered on belligerence, frustration rapidly veered into rage, and an infantile mean streak showed up.

One night, exhausted physically and gutted emotionally but putting on my best face, we were all trying to relax and settle into Christmas music and soothing holiday snacks. I was doing my best to re-create the feel of my childhood Christmases, and Mom just wasn't having it. She wouldn't sit still—she wanted this, then that, nothing satisfied her. She was clearly tired but refused to think about bed. At one point she grabbed a throw pillow and went to lie down on the hard wooden floor behind the couch, arguing that she wanted to sleep there and laughing when I insisted that it was not OK.

None of us knew how to handle this maddeningly impish version of her. I declared that everyone needed to go to bed, and Eric made himself scarce. He was as lost as the rest of us, likely embarrassed and afraid he'd go too far if he was the one to challenge her. I'd coaxed

her into her room, pleaded with her to put pajamas on, gotten her
to lie down, and started to tuck her in only for her to giggle, jump
out of bed, push me away, and run off like a toddler on a sugar rush.
She'd definitely had too much to drink, but I'd never seen this sort
of behavior. What do you do when your mother behaves like a
three-year-old? We were not in aging alcoholic territory anymore.
Something was clearly wrong.

One night when I had managed to get her down for bed, I cornered
Eric and my aunt in the kitchen, and we had *the talk*. Eric couldn't
deny it anymore. Having her out of her own home exacerbated all the
most extreme symptoms and robbed her of the ability to mask the
way she did at their house. I spent the rest of the visit wrestling with
my mother's temper and confusion, in the midst of my own unrav-
eling realizing that my mom, my sometimes best friend, sometimes
most maddening antagonist, was disappearing before my very eyes.

Over the next several months, she saw specialists of all sorts,
and we received the official news. She had dementia. They couldn't
diagnose the type yet, but it was already presenting as something
different from Alzheimer's, which was what had killed my gammy
(her mother) some six years earlier. She began medications to slow
the progression, and they told us the alcohol *had* to stop, as did the
smoking.

I recall Eric and I sighing and glancing at each other, wondering
how we were going to stop this woman from smoking and drinking
when our entire experience of her had always been punctuated by a
wine or martini glass in one hand and a cigarette in the other. In some
sort of twisted and beautiful gift from the universe, those two tasks
were actually the easiest. She was far enough along in her disease

progression that it was very much an out-of-sight, out-of-mind thing. She barely noticed the sudden lack of cigarettes, and Eric just put the wine and liquor out of her reach and poured her a single glass of nonalcoholic wine with dinner if she specifically asked for it.

Perhaps I'm giving her too little credit. Perhaps she really did exert some intentional willpower around giving up these two vices when her refusal to abandon either had been lifelong battles. Maybe she wanted so badly to slow or stop what was coming that she quietly resisted doing end runs around our removal of these things from her life while never seeking credit for the effort.

I don't recall how I spent New Year's Eve after that Christmas in 2007, that Christmas that I desperately wanted to be normal but wasn't. I just know that by the end of January 2008 Clint had moved out, and we'd taken the terrifying steps of breaking the news of our separation to our six-year-old son (who was blindsided and still bears the scars of that conversation, no matter how much we contorted ourselves to make it as palatable as possible). We told our families, our friends, and our neighbors. I think we both thought it might be temporary, but in reality once those scary conversations were had, once we'd revealed that the pretty picture I'd invested so much energy in painting hid a sometimes tortured and painful space, it felt right. We genuinely wished each other well, both of us eager to reconnect with ourselves and to try on the new identities waiting for us outside of marriage.

I certainly did not intend to almost immediately meet and shortly thereafter fall in love with the man who is now my spouse. Hell, I'd stressed to all my friends who thought Clint and I were both jumping into the wild new (to us) world of online dating a bit quickly that of course I wasn't going to get into a rebound relationship. I was just ready to have some fun! Famous last words being what they are, Dave and I now wonder at the timing of it all and our complete inability to imagine the improbable life we've built together since. Our love dawned on us like a morning we didn't expect to see, and to the surprise of everyone, we seized the day, and each other.

By the end of 2008, Chase was seven years old. I was winding down my divorce, and we'd just short sold the beautiful home we'd renovated and moved into one year before, its value having plummeted almost before the renovations were completed, as the economy faltered and then burst. I had been let go from the miserable big law firm job where I'd struggled to find meaning and grind out my days in six-minute billable increments. Though I made good money, I was buried in debt and was living paycheck to paycheck. Losing my job literally meant I couldn't afford my rent the following month, and I had moved in with Dave, almost everyone gasping at the apparent irresponsibility of such a move.

It seemed every decision I made that year was big, and bold, and tinged with desperation. I was a divorce attorney breaking all the rules I set for my clients, blending families with my boyfriend and his twelve-year-old son, Max, and nine-year-old daughter, Abby, less than a year after separating from Clint. Grasping at the threads of my old life, I was terrified I was making all the wrong leaps as I dealt with the scrutiny and approbation of friends and family who thought my marriage with Clint had been perfect and that I was creating chaos for the fun of it.

So, for Christmas of 2008, Mom and Eric came and stayed with us in my boyfriend's home, every detail completely upended from the year before. We all spent that week in varying stages of panic. Mom was overwhelmed by the noise and physicality of a home with three kids in it. Dave has always been a delightfully boisterous man, but to my mother he was utterly overwhelming.

I remember Mom staring at me wide eyed at the kitchen table, hands over her ears, confused. "Why is it so loud here?" she whispered. I rubbed her arm and kissed her forehead and said I knew it was different. That it was a lot for me, too, but that she had to trust there was a lot of love mixed in with the noise. The lonely only child in me reveled in this house full of shouts and laughter, but it wearied me, too, and I could tell the addition of another new space and more new people in my mom's orbit was not helping, even though progression had slowed a bit now that doctors were involved and we'd helped her make lifestyle changes.

I desperately wanted her approval that Christmas. I wanted her to reassure me that the sudden and whole changes in direction I'd made that year were valid. But I also knew I'd never have it, because the woman whose approval I craved was already missing. Her lucidity was still relatively present (or her ability to mask was), but when it slipped away, it was frightening.

It was our first Christmas with the three kids under one roof, kids who a year before hadn't known each other existed, or, in the case of my son, that his family was about to splinter. I went from being an only-child mom to juggling three children and all their personalities and activities. Both Dave and I had fifty-fifty parenting plans, so I had stepped into bonus parent duties beyond an every-other-weekend level right away. I had officially started my solo family law practice but had no money or energy to launch it, so I was essentially unemployed, handling just a handful of cases that first year that came to me from referrals. I dove into being a domestic partner with gusto even though that had never been a role I'd sought. I wanted to make things and create traditions and give gifts to cement the bonds we hoped would grow naturally over time. To soften the sharp edge of change that had torn so much from all of us in the prior year.

I desperately wanted my mother, my whole mother. My cantankerous, laughing, witty, judgy, critical, self-righteous, hilarious, generous mother. I had to content myself with glimpses here and there amid repeated and shocking evidence of her absence.

She was dismayed by all the change, worried about me and Chase, and worried about her own prognosis. She wanted to be helpful, and I realized that I had the perfect job for her. There were so many presents that year to go under the tree. And they all needed to be wrapped. Wrapping presents was one of my mom's superpowers. My entire life I'd watched her throw everything into the presentation of a gift. She wrapped with the sharpest corners, the paper perfectly measured and cut. She'd make absurd confections on top with bows and curling ribbon tumbling everywhere so you had to brush it aside to find the gift tags. I set her up with rolls of wrapping paper, tape, scissors, and ribbon. I made sure all the presents were in uniform boxes so there were no strange shapes, just rectangles and squares, and I wrote the names of the recipients on the boxes.

She was delighted. This was something she loved to do and could do well. About fifteen or twenty minutes later, I walked back to the doorway and saw her standing there, distraught. She panicked when she saw me. She had cut some paper, but in odd triangular shapes, none of the pieces big enough to wrap a single box. The pieces were strewn about, seemingly at random, littering the table and floor. She was trying to pull the edges of one piece of gift wrap together around a box and couldn't seem to understand why she couldn't get them to meet. Bits of tape were stuck in random places, and she handled the scissors like she'd never used them before. She was utterly adrift. It was such a tangible sign of what she was losing, of how her brain was betraying her, that she could not mask it or cover it or hide it. The misshapen, too-small pieces of paper were like the parts of her brain that weren't stretching to fill the gaps anymore. I felt horrid for having set up a scenario that in hindsight seemed designed to show her just how limited she had already become.

I leaped into the scene, giving her a face-saving excuse about needing her in the kitchen, distracting her, and turning her away from the horror of the loss as quickly as I could. I remember her shoulders slumping under my touch as I took her hand and led her from the room, away from the wreckage that seemed to be all that was left of her joy in giving gifts.

The caretaking began in earnest. Eric and I became collaborators, behind-the-scenes schemers. They were still five hours away, but, to give Eric a break, I began a pattern of flying or driving to spend long weekends with them every four to six weeks. For a while she continued being at home alone during the days, but she was lonely. She had no community or place to walk where people talked to her. The isolation was damaging, but Eric was stubborn, he wanted to keep her close and safe and resisted each step as long as he could.

Gradually we went through the stages, part-time help during the day to keep her company and out of trouble, and to do light house-keeping that she could no longer manage. Reading, the thing that had occupied such a huge percentage of her waking hours, became impossible for her. She couldn't track the words, so she'd get frustrated and quit trying to do anything other than occasionally thumb through a magazine. She became addicted to CNN, the noise and stimulation a constant barrage, but one that perhaps made her feel she was still connected to the outside world. We set up her cell phone (a simple flip phone) so that Eric and I were on speed dial. He was still working full-time, and my solo family law practice had become an actual full-time job by 2010, but we both had special ringtones for her, and we both picked up every time it was possible. Sometimes that meant I talked to her sixteen times in a day, usually about the same two or three things.

Eventually the part-time help became full time. She still called both of us constantly during our work days, and then when Eric got home, the help would leave, and he'd have to mind her till the help returned the next day. They got into routines that worked, and then she'd slip some more. I encouraged Eric to take respite time whenever I was there and wondered at how he was coping. I loved to make her laugh and help her find bits of unexpected joy in her day, but caring for her was an exhausting endeavor fraught with conflict and frustration. She had a wonderful counselor who came to the house and worked with her twice a week, and she agreed with me that Mom needed more stimulation and social interaction and access to physical and occupational therapy, but Eric didn't want to let her go to assisted living. As her husband, his say was final, and we spent a year quietly but earnestly arguing about it, trying to stay out of her earshot, covering and changing the subject when we slipped up.

The most unexpected parts of Mom's dance with dementia were

the delusions and hallucinations. Her therapist could explain some of it. For example, the person she saw in mirrors was unrecognizable to her because her image of herself had regressed to when she was much younger. Initially her confusion about this strange person who seemed to always be in the house with her, reflected everywhere in mirrors and windows, elicited the kindness and curiosity and generosity with which she'd always approached meeting new people.

Mom decided her name was Jane, and she set about nurturing her as she had once done with any of the folks she'd taken in over the years—her "strays" as she sometimes called them. She worried that Jane seemed too thin (my mother, who had fought with herself over her weight her entire life and had spent much of it fat, wasn't anymore; as her brain disintegrated, her body dissipated so that she was suddenly small and frail). She wanted to feed Jane. With the kitchen Mom-proofed, all she could access when the helper was otherwise engaged were snacks and cereal. For a while she'd make Jane a bowl of cereal and put it on the floor at the end of the hall, where the full-length mirror was, whenever she thought Jane looked hungry. Later the bowl would be empty, but Jane didn't ever seem to gain weight. The dogs failed to speak up about this, finding it to be a delightful addition to *their* day.

But Jane also never said thank you, or spoke at all. Rather than deciding Jane was rude, Mom decided Jane was being abused by her husband, and that they lived in the basement (there wasn't one) under the house. She became fixated on helping Jane, and then frustrated that Jane wouldn't do as she suggested. When I was with her, I tried to lean into her reality, as I'd read in all the caregiving advice articles, so I didn't try to convince her that Jane wasn't real, or that she was looking at her own reflection. I tried to suggest other explanations, but it was always a circular trip through madness.

As neither I nor Eric could take any of the physical actions she wanted us to, such as calling the police or making an official report, she began to suspect that we might be in cahoots with Jane's husband. As the disease progressed, her paranoia became a larger and larger feature. She lost the ability to navigate the house, constantly getting lost. Even though it was a single-story, simple home, she decided there were secret rooms full of cubicles where Eric was running a brothel. Sometimes she thought Eric was in cahoots with Jane's husband and that he was plotting to kill her or, rather more graphically, skin her alive. The last time we visited her in her own home, it was Thanksgiving, and we called ahead to say we were on our way. She grabbed the phone from Eric, screaming that he was sharpening knives (there was a turkey to carve) and pleading with me not to bring the children, because he was going to murder us all.

When I would walk in the door, I became her touchstone, and she would calm down. She rarely could maintain the darkest paranoid delusions in my presence, and having the kids around (bless their patience, I know they were freaked by her outbursts) made her happy. I remember, after all the drama about our imminent violent demise at the hands of her beloved, how she laughed with delight at the presence of people at her table, eating and talking like the old days. I wish we could have given her more of that. I wish they'd never left Atlanta, or that they'd come back. I cannot hold on to anger for Eric, though, just sadness that we lacked the skills and the foresight to navigate things differently than we did.

I'm so sorry, Mom. You were a hot contradictory stubborn mess, but when you needed us to be kind and to put you first, each of us failed in enough small ways that we lost you. Knowing that the losing would in all likelihood have happened anyway does not make it easier.

Chapter Two

FINDING MEANING IN MY MOM'S JOURNEY

I RECENTLY HEARD AN INTERVIEW BRENÉ BROWN DID with David Kessler in which they talked about the sixth stage of grief, one that he postulated after losing his research and writing partner Elisabeth Kübler-Ross, and one that crystalized for him after he lost his youngest son unexpectedly. While he was clear that the stages are never as linear as we would like them to be (denial, anger, bargaining, depression, and acceptance), and that they are not a gauntlet that you ever get to the end of, he also spoke of how living the truth of a sixth stage gave him a bit of a softening around the edges of his pain, a place to rest in his grief.

That sixth stage is finding meaning. Not in the death itself, but in how you respond to it, how it changes you, and in the difference that the person's life made. He said he realized that even in the midst of the most unimaginable pain, a pain that he had counseled countless parents through but had really not understood until he was in the midst of it himself, that he was able to see that not having ever known his son would have been worse than grieving his loss, and that was the starting point to finding the meaning that made it all bearable. Not better. Neither his loss, nor the loss of my mother, will ever be worth the meaning that we found in them. The blessings hidden in tragedy never make the event less tragic, but it does give us something with which to move forward.

For me, the meaning in my mother's diagnosis and death was a gift from her to me. Not one I wish she'd given me, but one that she most certainly did. She was a woman to whom things happened, a woman who lived reactively, who was buffeted by life's winds and never seemed—to me anyway—to entirely have understood who she really was or of what she was made, but who through it all, through the rages that overtook her and the addictions that sapped her, still operated with a large and open heart. A gentle thrum of kindness always underpinned the noise of her emotional volatility.

My mother's fears and lack of understanding of who she really was or how much she, and her own desires, actually mattered, led to a lifetime of procrastination—the kind of procrastination that robs us of life itself. When she wanted something, she made endless plans to pursue it sometime in the future. Almost never now. When she lost weight, when I didn't need her so much, when her husband didn't need her so much, when they retired, when they had a certain amount of money, etcetera, etcetera, etcetera. She was fearful of much, and rarely challenged her fears. She believed her desires were infinitely available to her, not recognizing that neglected somedays turn into nevers.

I can now see she'd spent her life punishing herself for not being who her parents expected her to be. Instead of graduating from college, she'd gotten pregnant. Her parents (purportedly to protect her younger sister's reputation, but probably also out of pride) put her on a train to Atlanta, and she was installed at a Florence Crittenton home, part of the great Baby Scoop era. She suffered through a pregnancy and closed adoption with no voice of her own, no opportunity to grieve or process her loss of that child, a loss over which she had no control. She met my father while she was pregnant with my unknown older half brother. My grandparents were liberal, intellectual elites, and their beloved oldest daughter was marrying a high school dropout who raced motocross. Underneath their sometimes high-handedness, though, my grandparents were kind and optimistic people. My mother's gracious heart had grown from their example, and they embraced my father, their marriage, and, later, me, with hopeful generosity.

Once I was born, my mom was unable to curb my father's penchant for escapism (through adrenaline and women), and her life became wholly centered on mine. She was not a helicopter mom in the modern sense. I spent whole days running wild outside with a pack of friends, climbing trees, building forts on the edge of the landfill in the woods behind the condominium complex where my earliest social memories were made, smoking cigarette butts collected from our homes and contributing them to the common stash. But she knew early on that she needed to be self-reliant, so she hustled.

Always looking for the next opportunity to grow, in the late seventies she'd scored high on an aptitude test that gave her access to training as a COBOL programmer. This propelled her from a dead-end job in the check-reconcilement department at a large bank to a twenty-year career in computer programming and project management.

Through this career she met Eric on the opposing team of a department Trivial Pursuit tournament. He was awkward and geeky but romantic and kind, and they adored each other. They left loving notes for each other all over the house when I was a teenager, rolling my eyes and making gagging noises at every opportunity. I believe my mom was really happy for a time, as happy as she ever was, when I was in high school. She was well respected at work, and they were comfortable financially—not wealthy, but able to buy the nice things she loved. Antiques and art glass, neon, and new wallpaper or dishes.

Still, even in the midst of her general contentment, she despised her own body and was endlessly angry at herself for being fat, and always worried that I would be too. Eric did his best to inoculate her from self recrimination—by loving her without condition—and I do think it helped her find some peace, although I never knew her to comfortably don a bathing suit. When I stumbled into adolescence with a figure that turned heads, she loved buying me clothes and letting me be edgy and artistic and expressive in the way I dressed. When I cut my hair short for the latter half of high school, she would bleach and dye it for me, in the kitchen with me perched on a stool, wearing a garbage bag while spilling all the latest drama and gossip from school.

My mom was the cool mom. My friends loved hanging out at my house, and she was never happier than when we were gathered around the coffee table making her laugh with our antics while she sat curled up in her seat at one end of the couch, a martini in one hand, a cigarette in the other, a beloved dog underfoot, Eric coming in and out while he made something delicious in the kitchen, ensuring her cocktail never ran dry.

Straddling the two worlds between my mother's home and my father's was like stepping in and out of a looking glass. I don't know if I was intrinsically a chameleon, able to color and shape-shift to fit into wildly varying environments, or if it was simply something that I learned growing up between two homes and worlds. My mother craved stability and consistency and got her thrills by buying objects that she could touch and display and talk about. My father was a wanderer in every sense of the word, always looking for the next adventure, the next relationship, the next idea, the next rush. He'd raced motorcycles and then worked in a Suzuki dealership. He loves Formula One and all things aviation. He doggedly showed up at the Delta Air Lines recruitment office every day for six straight weeks until they hired him, initially as a baggage handler. He spent thirty years there, ending his career as part of the exclusive and small Super Tug team. Sometimes on a Friday he'd pick me up from school on his motorcycle, earning me hella street cred from the other kids when I pulled my own helmet out of my locker and expertly hopped on the back of his bike, popping down the foot pegs with practiced nonchalance.

I'd keep a dress at his house, and we'd get up at the crack of dawn on Saturday, dress up (he had only one suit, a tan one, that he accessorized with the latest Delta Employee anniversary tie pin he'd earned for his years of service), drive to the airport, park in the employee lot, take the employee shuttle into the terminal, go to a customer service desk, and find out what planes had seats open for us that morning, preferably in first class.

Most of these were day trips. We'd fly to the Bahamas for the day, or Florida, or Washington, DC. We'd explore museums and beaches, rent cars and drive through towns. Sometimes we'd get stuck somewhere for a night, and we'd stay in crummy airport motels, where we'd watch black-and-white TV and laugh ourselves silly at the coin-operated vibrating beds that were in some of them. If we stayed home, he'd take me to visit old friends from his motorcycle gang days, guys who hadn't gotten their lives together like he had but whom he still loved and who doted on me during visits from this bright-eyed child who thought they were cool.

I remember one who played Joan Jett records for me and taught me to sing on key, helping me land a solo in the seventh-grade musical that year. We'd go into the city and eat at The Varsity, savoring the iconic greasy burgers and chili dogs for which they are famous, long past when I should have been in bed. We'd go to small airstrips to watch the planes or to ride in gliders. My dad signed up for skydiving lessons and I'd tag along, one time running back to the hangar for help when one of the sky divers hit a tree instead of his landing zone, immensely grateful that my dad knew I could be trusted with such an important task.

Dad and I raced go-karts and chased hot-air balloons. He taught me to ride a motorcycle (a small dirt bike that a friend had on his land) and left me to lie in the tall grass, staring at the clouds, wondering if I'd died when I flipped over the handle bars the first time, laughing at me when I got indignant that he hadn't run to my rescue. He loved to say, "Life is a smorgasbord, and if you are still hungry when you get to the end of the line, it's your own fault."

It gave me whiplash to come home from the freedom that my

dad represented to a mom who was often controlling, judgmental, self-righteous, and angry, but who was also kind and funny and generous and artistic. I'm sad for the person she might have been if she had allowed herself to simply be, if she had reached for the same acceptance of self that she routinely offered to others. The lessons from our parents that linger the longest, that bury themselves the deepest, are the unspoken and often unacknowledged ones. In all the lessons my mom sought to teach me growing up, the lesson to loathe myself and punish myself underpinned all the lessons of tolerance and understanding for others.

And so, when she was first diagnosed, it became startlingly and unremittingly clear to her that all the things, *all* of them, that she had always said she'd do someday were now out of reach. During one of her last visits to Atlanta, I found her crying and alone in the living room. We'd never been a physically affectionate family and rarely hugged, but I couldn't keep that distance in that moment. When I sat down and awkwardly put my arms around her, she collapsed into me, sobbing. She cried for all the things she'd never do, and she talked about how angry she was at herself for always putting everything off, for taking it all for granted. As her fear and despair buffeted against my body, I felt a fear of my own begin to take hold. I'd been busy juggling all the life around me, focusing on the kids and their needs, trying to grow my practice and grow in my profession, reassuring myself that someday, someday, I'd have time to do the things that I almost forgot were there, those dreams for adventure and spontaneity that still glimmered in deep recesses, pilot lights starved for air. I recognized that my somedays could become my mother's somedays, and that she'd given me the gift of that awareness while I still had time.

She was sixty-two when we moved her into assisted living. Once again I had to step into her delusions to help with the move. We told her that we were bringing in professionals to help Jane and to move the sinister people she feared were plotting her murder and corrupting her husband. We had visited the facility with her, and she liked the idea of being around people. She liked the garden, but she kept telling me she wasn't old enough. The sight of so many people ten to twenty years older than her shocked her, and she *did* look out of place, initially.

I did everything I could to make her room bright and familiar, with her favorite pictures and paintings, a cheery red love seat that turned into a bed so I could visit and stay the night. The evening before the move, after we'd finally gotten her down to bed, I found Eric sobbing in the home office. His stoicism shattered, he knew he would never again hold his wife in their own bed. *This is the worst night of my life*, he said.

I could only cry with him. I could find no words of comfort, no hope on the horizon. Walking her into her new home the next day was like leading a small and mistrustful child. She pulled back on our hands, resisting the walk from the car ever so slightly. But we kept reassuring her that this was just for now, that it was necessary to help Jane back at the house. She trusted us in the end, long enough to get her into her room.

Some of her neighbors stopped by to welcome her with a snack basket, and one of them had a dog, which delighted her. I reassured her that I'd stay till she was settled for the night. As I helped her get ready for bed and we walked into the bathroom, she saw Jane in the mirror, and I realized the critical error I'd made in not having them remove or cover that mirror. In that moment she panicked, realizing that something didn't make sense in the story we'd told her. If she was only there so that professionals could help Jane back at the house, why had Jane followed her?

She stared in horror at her reflection and then turned in anger on me, the recognition of betrayal in her eyes a searing blade in my gut. I don't remember all that I said to calm her, but somehow I got her redirected and into her pajamas and tucked into bed. She was becoming easier to redirect at that point, and I was the parent, and that was my job. She was scared, but she wrapped her arms around me when I leaned down to kiss her good night. I kept promising that I would stay till she was asleep, no matter how long it took. And so I did, tucked into the love seat in the darkened room, watching her breathe by a nightlight until her breathing slowed and her soft snoring began. I hoped that the social stimulation that would begin the next day when they came to lead her to breakfast would distract her from what this moment actually meant, and would justify our decision to move her.

Whether it was the loss of the familiarity of home, even the deluded version of home she'd been living in, or simply a matter of timing, she rapidly declined, necessitating a move to the locked memory care wing in a matter of months. Over the next two years her body stiffened into contorted shapes, and she lost the ability to walk or feed herself. I visited as often as I could, staying with Eric but spending time with her during my days there. Eric visited almost daily, regularly baking for the staff to show his gratitude for their care. She'd beg me to kill her on most visits, to release her from the indignity and confusion. I was relieved when those requests stopped, even though they likely stopped because she no longer knew who I was and had ceased remembering enough to be angry about being there.

Eventually she stopped making sense altogether. This kind, gregarious woman who loved nothing more than conversation and laughter lost the ability to speak coherently. Near the end, she seemed finally content, too far gone to remember what she'd lost. She'd smile and sway when I played her favorite music, leaning forward eagerly for spoonfuls of chocolate mousse, the sight of which always made her light up. She died a month before her sixty-fifth birthday. I was grateful to be awake for her last breath. To sit and anticipate a last breath for an hour or two is hard. I did it for days (initially alone and then with my aunt at my side), entering that trance-like space that encompasses all entrances and exits from this life. It was similar to a birth in the waiting and the hope. I am not ashamed to say it was a relief when, at last, her next breath didn't come.

In the following weeks I was consumed with all the details. We held a service in Atlanta, an intimate affair with the people who mattered. I think she would have been pleased with the service and my eulogy. I still have her cremains in the beautiful urn we picked out. It's swirling art glass, gold with the colors of peacock feathers, and it sits on top of our wine fridge. I like to think she listens to all that is happening in the heart of our home. When the lights flicker or things fall down and I'm alone in the house, I greet her cheerfully and search my heart for anything she might be trying to say.

When all the tasks of closing the last pages on a life were done, Dave and I sat down to talk about all of it. I'd now lost my mother and her mother (not to mention my dad's father) to dementia. My mother's had presented when she was alarmingly young. I had already lived a life full of adventures that my mother never understood, but my appetite for more was strong.

I was forty-two that summer of Mom's death. As I saw it, it was time to start living like I had an expiration date at fifty-five. So we talked about what I wanted to do with the thirteen or so years directly ahead of us. Travel was an obvious yes, and finally getting a breast reduction was also high on the list. I looked back over my life to that point and realized that all the most amazing memories involved saying yes to something that scared me, or at least made me feel uncomfortable. I realized that I was happiest when I was learning something new. It was hard to think about Dave losing me the way Eric had lost Mom, for both of us. But he embraced the idea of not wasting the gift Mom had given me. He pledged to support me through all the yeses I could imagine, to have my back and to build memories that perhaps only one of us would get to keep. We held each other, we cried, we laughed, and we agreed that we were going to take Mom's final gift and run with it. We got down to the brass tacks of living large.

Chapter Three

ᛒELONGING IN ᛒMY ᛒODY

O NCE UPON A TIME I DANCED. I DANCED IN DANCE STUDIOS for children, ballet, jazz, and tap. Modern. Modern made no sense till I was older, in college, when I began to understand the importance of the core, not just the muscles of the core, but the *core* of the core. The concept that there might actually be something central and solid and unchanging in my chameleon body and soul. I loved performing. I loved being backstage, I loved the chaos and the lights and the special treatment given to my hair and face. The costumes, the sequins, the tulle, the satin. I loved standing in a line of identical little girls, with hair in buns and bodies clad in satin leaves for our number, the teenage male soloist playing the part of Jack Frost in our recital about the seasons. I loved feeling like I belonged.

But I also danced alone. I was an only child who thought if only I had siblings, I wouldn't be so lonely. I was an only child who changed schools every year until third grade, then again during fifth grade.

Then again before sixth. I spent a lot of time in intense conversation with inanimate objects. I was smart and precocious and had the vocabulary of a forty-two-year old by the age of nine. My closest friends were my mother's friends. They were the only real constants in my life other than my parents. Other children were frequently loud and silly and inscrutable and annoying and intimidating. I found jewels among them, but they never lasted long, and few of them have endured in my memory.

And so I danced with an imaginary cast of characters. In costume whenever possible. I recall visiting my grandparents when my uncle was home from college. He was a classical guitarist and a stoner. He'd sit in his room for hours playing complex and cerebral acoustic pieces. His room had two doors, one to the Jack-and-Jill bathroom that connected his room to my aunt's old room, where I stayed, and the other to the hallway. I'd endlessly loop through his room, interpreting the music through movement. We wouldn't talk; it was just this unspoken mutual respect for our improvisational artistic souls and the way we could converse through the music. I had no self-consciousness in those moments, absolutely no concern for how my movement looked, but only for what it expressed. I'd move myself to tears at times, and both of us to laughter at others.

At the hippie private school my grandparents paid for right after my parents split up (because my mom couldn't afford to live in a good school district), I was regularly the last kid picked up from aftercare. I don't bear any anger around this; my mother worked hard and her work was unpredictable. She was one of the first people I ever encountered who had a pager who wasn't a doctor (not that we knew any doctors back then). To the contrary, when I was the last one there—or the last in my age group, anyway—I'd get permission to go to the small playground intended for the younger kids, and I'd dig out a red velvet dress from the dress-up box, and off I'd run, holding the skirt up so as to not trip. I loved that playground because part of it was made to look like a castle, and another part like a fire engine.

When I could get hold of the red velvet dress, I always gravitated to the castle. And there I would dance. Again without an ounce of self-consciousness. With no regard for eyes or the picture I might have made for beleaguered adults driving past at the end of their workdays, the tasks of the evening and family looming over them. I would make elaborate speeches and act out dramas. And when I say drama, I mean *drama*. I loved to play in the extremes of emotion. Acting out my own tragic demise. Or the demise of my prince. Or of my child. I was a martyr sometimes, a protector, a defender of the helpless. I ran and wheeled and fell and jumped and got the dress dirty and brushed it off and got my face dirty and didn't notice and let my hair dance itself into rats' nests that made my mother shake her head but also made her smile a little.

I can't imagine a time that my mother wasn't self-conscious, but surely she must have been—some day long ago, when she herself was a child. I think she was pleased with my freedom then. It didn't last, of course. At some point she had to start telling me to act my age, but there was a window there, before the storm of adolescence began, that I think she was happy to see me dance without a discernible beat, direction, choreography, or even an audience. I think the pure indulgence of dancing alone outside in a bedraggled red velvet dress-up-box hand-me-down without a care of who might see me made her feel lighter.

At the time I only knew I was at home. In my body. With myself. With the earth. Among my imagined cast of characters and villains and bosom friends who never said surprising things nor failed to understand my vocabulary nor teased me for talking funny.

When I was alone and free to move like that, I was also free from fitting in. I already knew I was a chameleon, but at that point in my life I had no idea if my chameleon qualities were evidence of good or evil. Whether my ability to blend in to any environment was a sign of my maturity and social skill or proof that I had no core, that I was nothing but an actor and manipulator without a solid center or sense of self. Being alone with my movement meant there were no layers keeping me from myself.

Chapter Four

BUDDING BETRAYAL

NCE UPON A TIME, I DANCED. THEN, SOMETIME, somewhere, my body and I were torn apart. It happened, as it does for so many, sometime during adolescence. There were so many forces intent on that result. Some of those forces were violent and predatory. Some were just present, and it was only in interaction with the other forces that they became destructive. Some were loving and acting to save me with the only tools they had or knew.

There were the grown men who drew attention to how my body made *them* feel. A dinner guest who, when he encountered me alone in the kitchen, asked how I enjoyed my budding breasts, breasts that till that moment I hadn't realized were noticeable in my clothes. In that moment he made it impossible to ever again be unconscious of how they looked. That offhand comment, as creepy as I now know it was (and knew then because of the shame it made me feel, the redness that came to my face—I was ten or eleven), marked a moment where

I became fixated on how my breasts looked, whether they were too obvious, whether they were being shown to advantage, whether they bounced too much. From that day on I insisted on bras all the time, preferably minimizing ones.

There were the grown men who communicated their attraction to me before they realized how young I was. The ones who, if they didn't actually seem a bit revolted with themselves when they did realize my age, at least withdrew and didn't continue to pursue me. They reinforced the idea that how I looked mattered more than just about anything. And also that how I looked carried a power that was enticing, and exciting, and scary, and a bit addictive.

There were the grown women who gushed over how blessed I was with my full breasts (C cup by the time I turned thirteen). Who said they wished they had been as lucky. Who joked that I had it made with my hourglass figure and that I'd forever make other women jealous. These same grown women weren't around in PE when any sort of physical activity made much of the class stare and titter. They didn't see the PE teachers who rolled their eyes when I complained of a stomach ache every chance I got to avoid having to do anything to call attention to the way these two parts of my body moved.

I had never liked sports involving balls. My mom was not athletic, and my dad was into motor sports, so there had never been any inclination by either of them to sign me up for team sports. Dance was my sport. Dodgeball and volleyball in PE class, hell, even kickball, were torture. I couldn't throw and catch, and on top of it all, when I was forced to participate, everyone stared not just to see how inept I was but to see how my breasts would bounce around in the process.

There were the beloved family members (some of the same women who told me how jealous they were of my shape and how lucky I was) who began to drill into me that I had to be extra careful. Mindful of how I dressed. Mindful of how I moved. Mindful of whom I chose to be around and where. It became clear to me that this body of mine, for all that it was celebrated, was also something that elicited strong reactions from almost everyone around me and made it impossible for them to see *me*, to engage with *me*.

My elderly pediatrician, nearing retirement, complimented me for having the same measurements as Marilyn Monroe. My physics teacher in a special program I did in eighth grade for extra-smart science students leered a bit when he handed back my lab notebook, noting that I extrapolated curves better than anyone else in the class. To his credit he immediately looked ashamed for saying it and was awkward and avoided meeting my eyes the rest of the one week I was in his classroom. I recall feeling bad for *him*, even as I turned the anecdote into a funny story to illustrate just how "cool" and impervious I was to unwelcome objectification. I knew I earned an A for the work I did in that class, but hey, what's the harm in an extra edge, right? I recognized that many people I encountered were simply not interested in what lay beneath my skin; my shape was my value. I was a prize or a target. An object first and foremost.

I very much liked being the center of attention, and always had. In second grade, before the shape-shifting began in earnest, I went to a writing workshop organized by my school. I wrote about visiting my great-grandmother in a nursing home. My beloved grandfather's mother, demented and in the fog of senility, bitter and bombastic and full of unrestrained rage. She wasn't doing well. I think my grandfather knew her time was near, and he wanted her to see me, the great-granddaughter he doted on so completely. He was so proud of me, so loving, so indulgent. But I remember when we got out of the car there was a tension in his body that was utterly strange to me. He was a professor, a clinical psychologist, a man who belonged to and led organizations in his community and was written about in the local paper. I could not comprehend him being fearful of anything, but his fear was what I felt as we approached the building.

I wrote about the smell of urine and bleach making my eyes sting as we entered. The way his voice sounded like a child's as we entered the door to her room as he pushed me forward, proud of this small intelligent person he had helped raise, seeking his mother's approval. She exploded in vitriol. She screamed at me, her hair wild and her eyes blazing with hatred. I wrote about the old-lady cracking timbre of her voice as she railed at me to *Get out!*, spit flying from her lips.

Forty-two years or so later, my heart breaks for my grandfather. He got me out as quickly as he could, he held it together, he tried to explain, although I don't recall what he said. I think he went back in alone to try to calm her down, but either way we were back in the car no more than ten minutes after leaving it. I have no memory of how I processed that scene in the story I wrote, a story written when the experience was both still recent and when I had almost no context within which to process what had happened. I do know no one hugged me. We were never a hugging family. I do know I had been deeply shocked and frightened, and that I felt so sad for my granddaddy and did my best to reassure him that I was OK.

The writing teacher came to me as we were lining up to go back to the bus. She held my story, written in pen on lined paper with scratch outs and doodles. She put her hand on my shoulder and pleaded with me to grow up and write. To never stop writing. The intensity in her eyes scared me a bit. Maybe, maybe I *was* special. Maybe the familiarity of the changeling stories in my beloved fairy-tale books actually did mean something.

Then in fifth grade Mom put me in an acting class. I knew I wanted to act. I loved writing little skits and making up characters and performing them for my mother's adult friends, who would crack up and shake their heads in wonder at how completely I could embody these imaginary people in my world. I think she was feeling bad about uprooting me from my hippie private school in Atlanta to move to Florida with her boyfriend. I was well behaved but bored out of my mind in my new public school. She found an acting class offered by students at the Jacksonville University and enrolled me.

There were two students teaching us, and only three girls in the class. They found a script about three cheerleaders, and we performed it as part of their class, on a big stage at the university. Someone, after the one-time performance, perhaps their professor, pulled me aside backstage. She put her hand on my shoulder and pleaded with me to grow up and act. To never stop acting. Once again, this woman, this woman with authority and knowledge and age, had singled me out and demanded a promise, right then and there, solemnly and with feeling, to not let my talent languish.

And so I entered adolescence with the hopes and visions of these two strange women following me everywhere. And yet, all of a sudden, because I now had breasts, all else was no longer important. My breasts were the first and sometimes only things people began to notice about me. I got braces and learned that most of the time, if I kept my mouth shut, people assumed I was an adult. I turned heads and got smiles and winks and flirtatious comments.

My mother was torn between fear and pride. In some way, I think she was jealous of the way my body was intent on fulfilling some feminine ideal she had never felt in her own skin. When we shopped, she was excited for me to try on things that accentuated my figure, so long as it didn't veer into looking "slutty." I loved old Hollywood, though, and became obsessed with Marilyn Monroe because so many people said I looked like her. I changed identities daily in high school, sometimes wearing pencil skirts with seamed stockings and stilettos along with 1940s-style blouses with outrageous shoulder pads. Wearing one of these outfits while traveling with my father caused a stir when we encountered his wife's coworkers. His wife got a frantic call that he was having an affair and flaunting his mistress around the airport. My dad seemed to think the whole thing was pretty funny. I felt a strange mix of pride for having achieved the look I was going for and disgust that people couldn't still somehow tell I was his *kid*, for crying out loud.

On other days I wore punk rock T-shirts and Keds defiantly held together with duct tape, mismatched with a white eyelet lace petticoat and fingerless gloves. I embraced it all, the parachute pants, the berets, the boots, and the neon. The jellies and the Swatches.

In the end, no matter what I did, I existed in the twilight between childhood and adulthood, in a misty space filled with danger and opportunity. A place where I was the target of envy, anger, jealousy, disgust, lust, and sexual promise. All this for just existing. I desperately wanted to be seen, but again and again, being seen meant being sought. Being sought meant being used. Being used meant being derided. Being derided meant being blamed. Being blamed began the process of decoupling. I disconnected from my body. I left it.

Chapter Five

BREAKING UP WITH MY BODY

T BEGAN AS MOMENTS, JUST BRIEF MOMENTS OF dissociation from something happening to my body while my mind went elsewhere. But it ended with an almost total divorce. My body and I were like divorced parents, forced to communicate but more comfortable keeping that communication as minimal as possible. We passed messages, and I became extremely facile at ignoring most of the messages from my body. Pain became a disconnected thing that happened to my body and which at times required attention from my brain, but as little as I could manage to give it. Emotional pain, fear, sadness at the repeated realization that my body was frequently the only part anyone wanted to connect with, the loneliness of the once-whole child I had been before my breasts grew—that, well, the only answer for that was to take control. To become the one who chose not to let others know me rather than to allow others to decide for themselves.

While social programming is powerful all on its own and plays a big role in how humans raised as girls and women come to abandon a full occupancy of their own flesh, another thing that far too many of us have in common is actual trauma, often sexual (which is in itself already violent), and sometimes violent in other ways as well. I share in this legacy. I scarcely know any AFAB (Assigned Female at Birth) people who don't.

When I was fourteen, I was groped and slobbered upon by a man my aunt was dating (she had brought him over to my dad's house to introduce him to the family). Because I had held his eyes a little long when he stared, because part of me was thrilled to be looked at like a grown-up, because I had flipped my hair saucily, and because I was wearing makeup, I knew it was mostly my fault. He got scared when he heard someone coming up the stairs, and I locked him out of the room and never had to see him again. So no harm, no foul, right?

But then there was the date rape about six months later. My mom said I was too young for car dating, but this guy was my best friend's sister's friend and went to a different school. He was a nerd. He was unimposing with a slight build. He was smart and funny and had starred in the school musical. He'd won my parents over, and none of us could imagine this boy ever doing intentional harm.

In all actuality I had already lost my virginity, by choice, with a boy who actually asked for my consent at a time when that concept was utterly foreign in our culture (it was the mid eighties). That had not been a relationship, more a curious and precocious act on my part. But I thought that now that I was dating *this* boy, and he kept treating me with kid gloves, stopping after a brief make out, not wanting to push me too soon, that I should be honest with him. I don't know what I expected. Maybe a talk about what sex meant to each of us? When and how we might want to proceed?

I told him I wasn't a virgin. And everything changed. He was on top of me quickly, with only a brief pause and a quick, "This is OK, right?" I didn't answer. I just turned my face away from him, tears welling up and spilling onto my cheeks. Apparently he took that as a yes and proceeded. I hadn't wanted it, but it became really, really clear that not being a virgin meant that what I wanted maybe didn't matter, and that what I was good for had suddenly become a very small subset of who I was.

I pretended it was all OK after, even though I was in a good deal of pain. My body had not wanted the invasion any more than my mind or heart had. But he was my official boyfriend. Everyone liked him. He was a good kid, not the kind of guy who rapes people. And it couldn't have been rape, because I didn't say no, not explicitly. I didn't push him away. I didn't get out of the car while I still could. Hell, I'd still tried to kiss him good night even though he wouldn't look at me afterward, perhaps some part of his soul crying foul after the act was done.

I'd still tried to call him for weeks afterward while he dodged me. I was clearly trash. I went on to date other boys. I developed a reputation. Not all the boys were evil; it wasn't that simple. Most of them were as messed up as me, insecure and awkward and confused and traumatized in their own ways. The eighties were a hell of a time to be a teenager. Some of the boys threatened suicide if I didn't love them right. Some of them kissed and told. Some of them leered at me in front of company and cried when we were alone. My body was always the reason they wanted to be close to me in the first place. I began to wear my badge of sluttiness like armor. If that was all they wanted, it was all I wanted, too, and when they rejected me, it was just because of that, not because they actually knew me. Fuck them. Fuck the double standard. The young feminist in me burned bright. Why couldn't I be provocative *and* smart? Sexy *and* curious?

I was not *enjoying* the sex, though. Rather, it was a way for me to feel powerful. I certainly wasn't having orgasms or anything close to them. I told my body, which was crying out for tenderness and softness and slowness, that it was wrong to want those things. I wielded it like a weapon, against boys whom I hurt as much as those who had hurt me, and against myself. Penance perhaps.

When I got pregnant, there were two possible fathers. One of them swore that he was actually infertile, and it couldn't have been him (I was sixteen, and he was in college) and hung up on me. The other fretted and scraped together fifty dollars toward my abortion but otherwise melted out of my life. My body was what had brought them to the yard, so to speak, but when my body wasn't playing by their rules, it had no purpose, and therefore neither did I. It was a dirty thing, obviously, a shameful thing. I did not sink into despair, a point of misplaced and caustic pride until I learned that the battles I fought with my body (both against it and using it as a weapon) hurt me deepest of all in my quest to prove that I was not a victim.

In the first heady weeks of college I got invited to a house party at another college the next town over. A brand-new friend had a high school buddy who was an upper classmate there. He was hot, and an artist. We hung out all day, giving each other back rubs and flirting.

Everyone could tell we were hot for each other. As people started falling asleep or passing out, he led me to a back room. We started making out, but he was rougher than I wanted. I had, against all odds, landed a full scholarship to college and had thought I'd set a new pattern for myself—*not* be the school slut. I panicked and tried to back away from him, wanting to slow things down. I wasn't sure I wanted to actually have sex, have everyone in this house and my new college friend know that I was that girl you could hook up with at a party. He didn't get angry; he just didn't stop.

I started protesting in earnest. He held me down, pinned me, got me out of my clothes. I knew I *could* scream, call out, make some sort of noise. We were in a house full of people. But I didn't know any of them well, while they all knew him, and I was the outsider. They'd seen me flirting and touching him all day. If I did what I needed to do to get other people to stop this, then I'd forever be that *other* girl, the dreaded tease. Part of my brain did calculations as I kept trying to squirm away. What do I really have to lose? It's not like I'm virginal. If I just let him do it, it will be over faster. I won't cause a scene. I won't start college with the reputation of being a harpy. And so I willed myself to hold still, to pretend to be kinda into it, but he took freaking forever, tossing me around like a rag doll. I was so sore the next day I could barely walk, and my short cutoffs revealed bruised handprints on my thighs.

When my new friend and I got in my car to drive back to our campus, I caught her looking at them and shrugged it off. "I like it a little rough," I said, and we never spoke of it again. That time I *did* say no. That time I had tried to fight him off. But ultimately he'd worn me down, so obviously it wasn't rape. Obviously I'd asked for it. I even went so far as to ask him if he wanted to get together again. In hindsight I *needed* it to have been my choice to have sex, so I pretended it had been. But he wasn't interested. I pretended I didn't care. On some level I know my body was relieved that he'd not have access again, but my body and I weren't really speaking at that point.

I made it through college with some less traumatic but still underwhelming boyfriends, with a tortured long-distance relationship that for a time became an engagement (bless his heart, that was the first person with whom I *ever* shared an actual orgasm, so obviously I had to marry him since I couldn't imagine anyone else would ever unlock *that* secret), and I even had my first experiences with women and came out as bisexual. I was still drawn to unsatisfying and often painful one-night stands for reasons that made no sense at the time. They were almost never pleasurable, always unsatisfying, and never led to connection of any sort, between me and the other person or me and my own body, which grew more and more distant.

The year after graduation, while I was living in South Africa, I received an invitation to see a jazz band. The invitation came from a much older man, an uncle to the wife of the couple who was hosting me for a year of volunteer work. She had introduced him to me, and when he invited me out, I accepted because he was her family and was far too old for me, and I thought it was a group activity. She said nothing, and when he picked me up, he was alone.

He was in his sixties, ancient to me. The wife of the couple I was staying with sent me off with him, waving nicely, so when he admitted that no one else was coming, I went along with it. Thankfully he was a drunk, and ultimately that was what saved me. Even though he did his best to pin me down, he was sloppy and slurring, and I was younger and mad as fucking hell and I fought until he passed out. He'd taken me away from town, we were on an empty road on a mountainside, and I had no way to get home nor any idea how to get there. I'd rolled him back into the driver's seat and couldn't figure out how to get him out so I could just take the car (not to mention I hadn't yet mastered how to drive a right-hand-drive stick shift on left-hand-driving roads, and I wasn't entirely sober myself). So I'd had to wait, under the moonlight, staring out over the lights of the city, for some miserable period of time, for him to rouse enough to drive me home.

He'd lost his fight once he woke up, but was surly and rude. I had no illusions that I'd be treated fairly in this foreign infant country that was still writing its constitution. I realized that the wife of the couple I was staying with thought I was too independent for my own good, so I figured she'd side with him. Months and months later, when I was still haunted enough by nightmares about that night that I confided in her husband, I learned that she had been angry that I hadn't asked permission to go. In her culture, an unmarried young woman was not free to do as she pleased, and she resented my flouting a rule no one had explained to me. When I agreed to go with him, even though I thought he was harmless and that he was taking me to a concert with other harmless people, she decided that I needed to be taught a lesson for not asking her permission first as the woman of the house. Turns out he had a history of raping and sexually assaulting people, and she had every reason to know what he intended. Thankfully, by the time I learned of that betrayal, I was no longer living in her home or subject to her twisted efforts to teach me to be "respectable."

My sexual assault history is a story and dynamic as typical and mundane as any and is absolutely one of the most unspecial things about me. But it may also be one of the most typical and mundane and unspecial things about you. Because I finally understand now that I was not alone, that I was not deserving, that I was not damaged goods. You are not alone. You were not deserving. You are not damaged goods.

In the months of recovering from that final assault, finding my way in a foreign land, I met my first husband, Clint, the father of my son. He was kind and gentle, solicitous and generous, funny and sweet. He definitely made me feel desired physically and sexually, but he also wanted to know all of me, and to share his own wounds and the scars that had knit them closed. I could tell him anything, be my whole self without fear of judgment or recrimination. My pleasure was always a priority for him, and because we began dating when I was certain our relationship had no future, a certainty I reminded him of frequently, he treated time with me as precious and asked nothing of me but my attention and affection in the moment. I had no interest in a transatlantic and transhemispheric relationship and couldn't fathom that I'd want to make the kind of commitment at my age necessary to move someone to another country.

As my eventual return to the States approached, the thought of leaving him behind, this comfortable and soothing presence in my life, became unbearable. I extended my stay and then convinced myself that we were perfect for each other. At that stage of both of our lives, it was probably true. We married two weeks before I came home, and it took another seven months to get him through the immigration process. We had several years of contentment and happiness, supporting each other through our educations and our career wanderings. Exploring our world and finding a sense of home. I believe our wounds drew us together, and I believe our love worked a lot of healing for us both. In the end, however, we were also toxic to each other. I needed to be in control to feel safe, and he allowed me to be in charge, a trait I thought was absolutely necessary for my safety and happiness. After a decade, however, he was stifled and resentful, and I was exhausted and cranky. We both needed to be free of the behaviors we'd tried on and then solidified to the point where neither of us could breathe. I'm forever grateful to Clint, though, and still consider him family despite the fact we've been divorced now much longer than we were married. By the time our marriage splintered, I was still a long way from reconnecting with my body, but I was no longer weaponizing it or using others to hurt myself physically. And it was the pain of our impending split that led me toward those first steps of reconnection.

Chapter Six

RUNNING TOWARD RECONCILIATION

LATE ONE NIGHT IN THOSE SPLINTERING DAYS AT THE beginning of the end of my first marriage, I took a break from legal research on a case and found myself on Craigslist. I don't recall why, actually. I don't know what I thought I was looking for that day. I just knew that even though I loved every inch of our newly renovated home, it still felt like it didn't fit us, or we didn't fit it, and that we definitely didn't fit each other.

I know now that my biggest failure as a spouse in my first marriage was not that I didn't keep house right, or keep fit and healthy. It was that I refused to allow myself to be vulnerable. I needed to be in charge more than I needed to be myself. I left very little room for my husband to breathe, and, to be fair, at the time he lacked the skills he needed to take the space and air he deserved for himself, so we found ourselves in a place of fierce resentment and passive aggressiveness. Counseling helped to a point. It made us functional roommates, but that was it.

My need to be in control also meant that in my mind it was my job to fix it. Making more money hadn't done it. Building a better house hadn't done it. So I started to think that maybe fixing myself, my body, making myself younger and stronger might. Clint and I had tried to be healthier before, but I always gave up pretty quickly. I had asthma that, at the time, wasn't terribly well controlled, and exercise exacerbated it. I used that as a reason to avoid cardio at all costs. I knew I was getting fat, but I got tired of trying so hard. Being a mom, going to law school, making sure everyone believed we were a perfect family unit, was exhausting, and I decided that femininity was a burden I wanted to reject. I wore appropriate clothes, modest clothes. I stopped wearing makeup most of the time, I let go of contacts and went back to my sensible and boring eye glasses. My hair was its natural mousy color, and I did nothing to style it to any advantage. I did the bare minimum unless it was a special occasion and took every opportunity to collapse into the couch or into the bed, to move as little as possible.

Exercising hurt. It made it hard to breathe. It was embarrassing. I couldn't imagine ever dancing again. But that September night in 2007, cruising Craigslist, I stumbled across an interesting ad. It was from the founder of a company called Operation Boot Camp. He and his partner had developed this program and were franchising the concept. They needed a copywriter for their internet marketing, and they were willing to barter a free four-week boot camp session in exchange for some copywriting for their website. Boot camp?

That met at 5:45 a.m.? Outside? The entire idea seemed totally out of character for me, but I was so sad that night. I felt so alone. Something in the ad resonated, and I responded to it.

First I made sure to manage expectations by explaining how unfit I was and how I was probably not what they needed. I was shocked when I got a quick reply only a few minutes later. Could I manage to walk a mile? If so, then they could work with me. If I wanted to give it a shot, I could meet them the following week at 5:45 a.m. on a Monday morning in Candler Park, where their first franchisees would be starting their first session at that location. No charge, just show up, make it through that morning, and we'd talk.

I told him I would, and then I hit send, and then I think I laughed out loud at myself. What in the actual hell was I doing? Exercise, even moderate indoor exercise, was painful and scary to me. I was *not* outdoorsy at that stage of my life. Doing any sort of exercise that bore any resemblance to a tool the armed services uses to break the will of healthy young humans was clearly going to kill me. But as I shifted in my chair that night, trying to get comfortable, I realized how much pain I was already in. In that moment, I couldn't remember not being in pain. Something on my body ached or throbbed or pinched most of the time. Being out of breath was scary and frequent. My back always hurt. So, yeah, boot camp was going to hurt. But if I was avoiding exercise, if I was avoiding movement, because I wanted to avoid pain, the plan was failing miserably.

What if, I thought, *what if pain is inevitable?* We are sold painlessness our whole lives, but chasing a pain-free existence never works. You always have to trade some kind of pain for another. If that is true, and at the ripe old age of thirty-four, that certainly seemed to be coming true, then what if I could control the kind of pain? What if I could trade the pain of lethargy for the pain of growth?

I shook my head. It seemed simplistic, and as I heaved out of my chair that night, I didn't think I'd go. But I did, even though I had nothing to wear, no proper jog bra, no proper exercise shoes. I showed up that dark September morning. I was out of breath before we began, my heart beating out of my chest with fear. There were some other fearful folks, but almost everyone seemed fit already, awake, alert, confident. The two instructors greeted me kindly, Jojo knocking me back with the sheer force of her contagious joy, and Tim reassuring me with kind and knowing eyes, telling me even before he confirmed it with his words that he knew where I was, that he'd been there before, and that this was worth doing, and that he wouldn't let me do it alone.

The owners of the company, Jeff (who had been my Craigslist correspondent a few nights prior) and Heidi, both of them clearly in competition-level shape, were also there, but reserved, letting Jojo and Tim take their baby and launch it at this new location. The first day of every Operation Boot Camp session involved a warm-up (fifteen minutes of activity more intense to me than any I'd experienced outside of brief sexual interludes in the prior ten years, at least) and then a fitness test. It was standard gym class stuff. Running a timed mile. Counting the number of pushups and sit-ups and tricep dips (*tricep whats?*) you could complete in a minute. We set off on the mile "run," and I felt validated in the proof of my inadequacy as everyone pulled ahead of me and I found myself almost alone. *Almost* but for Heidi and Jeff. Ostensibly they wanted to hang with me to talk about the copywriting gig. They also had Heidi's fluffy bichon on a leash, so they weren't looking to race anyway, they said.

They talked about the writing stuff, and I may have responded. I don't recall. I do remember them glancing at each other and me, as I shuffled along, but not in a way that made me think they felt sorry for me. Rather, they seemed to see promise in my struggle. They acted like they had nowhere in the world they'd rather be than pretending to jog at what must have been a painfully slow pace for them, while I shuffled along, determined to not let my gait fall into something that could be called walking. It was the longest mile I'd ever traversed by any means. When at last we caught up to the group, they were already rested and comparing the times they'd written in the logbooks they'd given each of us to track our progress.

Impossibly, Jojo was still waiting with the stopwatch for me to cross the finish line, and even the most fit among the rest of the group cheered for me with gusto when I came into view. Even now, I wonder, *What if actual PE in school had been like that?* But it wasn't, and so here I was, at thirty-four, rewriting what should be a foundational memory.

My mile took me over seventeen minutes to "run." I met Jojo's high five, stumbled into the bushes, and vomited. When I stood, embarrassed, Tim was shielding me. He literally had my back, patting it and reassuring me that he'd done the exact same thing when he first started. I shook my head. That could not be possible. He smiled in the shy way he had, and I knew it was true. I wasn't alone here.

After I limped through the rest of the test, Heidi and Jeff solemnly told me they were willing to give this barter a try, that they believed that we had come together for a reason, that I was what they needed, and maybe, maybe Operation Boot Camp was what I needed. Jojo infected me with her smiles and literally leaped in the air in excitement when I said yes, yes, I'd come back the next day.

Clint was nonchalant about it. We'd been together long enough for him to watch me start countless new things, new projects, new hobbies, new interests, only to let them wither before anything came of them. It was a toxic self-immolating spiral that fed on itself. I had bought into the idea that to be a proper adult, one committed oneself to a career, a proper one, with benefits and dress codes and promotions. That one picked a hobby or a skill or two and developed and perfected them. That one did not flit about life alighting on this idea or that activity only to flit again and alight again, and again. It felt like a serious character flaw that I operated that way.

I know now there are valid reasons my brain worked like this, and still does. I've only recently been diagnosed with ADHD. I've only recently come to understand the programming that was incompatible with my brain and my very soul but to which I very eagerly cleaved, desperate to belong to the hallowed halls of productive adulthood, to be approved of by Protestant forebears whose names I didn't even know. But back then, each time I failed to finish or to continue the latest thing that caught my attention and my passion, it proved to me further the depravity of my personhood, the failure that I knew I was, even though I put on a good act. I didn't believe I had impostor syndrome, just that I was the *best* impostor and that eventually I'd be found out.

I don't know why it was different this time. Perhaps in some way the pain of boot camp was a sort of atonement that I craved for my obvious sins. Perhaps spiting Clint by sticking with it was at last a bit of passive aggressiveness that served me. The pain I felt the next morning was sharp, but it was just a month, right? Just four weeks. And they needed me. I'd committed to writing the copy, which I couldn't very well do without experiencing the product. In truth, that was likely the hook I needed. I was always better at showing up for others than I was for myself.

I'm a naturally curious person, and part of the magic of the boot camp process was that you never know what the workout will be that day. I'd never been part of a program that required me to surrender to whatever the instructors demanded, without any preview. Every morning I got better at breaking it down into steps and tackling the most immediate, without thinking further.

First it was the choice to actually get out of bed at 5:00 a.m. Well, I did have to pee, didn't I? And once I was up, I practiced putting my brain into autopilot, slipping into the workout clothes and the running shoes and filling my water bottle while my brain focused on something far beyond boot camp. Like, what was the dinner plan that night? What were my son's activities? What were my responsibilities at the office that day? Before I knew it, I'd be in the car. If it was really cold, I might pause, but then, well, I was already in the car, so it was silly not to drive the twelve minutes to Candler Park (an impossibly short span of time at any other time of day, but there are benefits to being on the road at 5:30 in the morning). And I might pause again before getting out of the car, but by then I'd see Jojo and Tim in the lights of the parking lot, radiating good will and energy and, well, they'd seen me by then, too, and it would be rude to just drive off. *I'll just do the warm-up,* I'd tell myself, *that's only fifteen minutes,* and then I could tell them my knee was bothering me and bail. But I never did. After the warm-up, they'd announce that day's workout, and that first month all of it was new, all of it required learning. So much of it was gamelike. It was a month of predawn field days but where no one was laughing and staring at my breasts bouncing, and where even the fittest and hottest people cheered for me like I'd just hit a home run even when I was the last one passing a baton or rounding a cone.

I'd also never, outside of childhood PE nightmares, worked out outside. We got dirty. We had no mats or towels. We worked out in all weather. The only things that might cause a cancellation were too much ice or too much lightning to be safe. Other than that, we did it all in the mugginess and in the rain, in the snow and in the wind. The grass was pretty much always wet that time of day, and the smell of my sweat and my rancid shoes mixed with grass and wild onion and loamy dirt and red clay. We slipped and fell and jumped and rolled. We were working out, hard, but we were also playing. The workouts were games, but without the hard edge of competition that had turned me off so much in school. They were collaborative games, where we all benefited from mutual encouragement and cheering.

I was right. I was right about the pain. All pain is not equal. The pain of sore muscles hard worked is infinitely better than the pain of lethargy and sloth. It is sometimes harder pain, sometimes sharper pain, but it is pain that changes you in ways that actually buoy the soul instead of defeating it. I still very much cared about how I looked and wished to lose weight, but pretty quickly I became more obsessed with improving my times and my abilities. My body came to life bit by bit that month. I caught myself laughing while running. While initially I cringed at the thought of getting dirty, by the end of that first month there was a workout that involved sprinting up a hill, then literally rolling down it, only to leap up and do it again. It was absurd, and I started laughing as I rolled in the wet grass, faster and faster, dreading the run back up but gleeful about the next roll back down, grass and pine straw stuck in my hair, dirt on my cheek, and the grin of an eight-year-old caught in the reflection of a nearby car window. And every time I didn't bail on the process, I felt a little more proud of myself, a little more healed, a little more strong. My brain and my body were finding each other again.

In the last week, we did a shorter-than-normal warm-up, and the instructors announced that the day's workout was called "Long Run." Usually the workouts had fun and sometimes punny names that alluded to the content. "Long Run" was arrestingly simple. And terrifying to me. Yes, running was part of every workout, but not continuous running, just short bursts as part of a choreography of movement. I remember feeling angry and disillusioned. This wasn't special or different. This was just going to be torture.

As I stood there, probably scowling (there was that eight-year-old coming out again), thinking about darting back to the safety of my car, Tim was suddenly by my side. "I have you," he said. "You can do this. You'll be slow, but I'll stay with you no matter what."

I sighed, and nodded, and we started. The leader had a light on their back, and a few others had lights as well, so even though Tim and I were what seemed like an eternity behind, we somehow had enough light to not lose them. Tim had already shared a bit about his journey with me, a journey that had started more than one hundred pounds heavier, that began with walking marathons. He knew about and understood my asthma, and how scary it was for me to feel out of breath, because for an asthmatic, feeling out of breath is sometimes associated with emergency rooms and anxious doctors. I'd never thought about that connection, or felt so seen or understood around that very private and particular fear. I had learned to measure and slow my exercise breathing since we'd started, even when my chest felt tight. To use my inhaler when needed but to not need it as much, because for me, anyway, my asthma, while fully a physical condition, could be influenced by my state of mind.

We were going to "run" until we stopped—that was all there was to it. And so I surrendered. About halfway through, with the lights of the leaders up ahead doing ovals in the street so that they didn't get completely out of sight, I realized that Tim and I were still talking. *Not* that Tim was talking and I was breathlessly nodding and grunting. I wasn't going on and on, but I was carrying on some level of a conversation while jogging over an extended period of time. *Huh,* I thought. *That's pretty neat.* Tim kept me focused on that conversation, and on understanding how amazing this body I'd ignored for decades actually was.

When we caught up to the rest of the group, done with the run and stretching, I got the "afterschool special" cheering again. I thought I'd grow tired of it, but it never felt less than genuine, and that eight-year-old grin came right back. I hadn't thought about the distance we'd run. Tim had kept my mind on other things, but someone had been wearing one of those newfangled GPS watches, and Jojo asked for them to read out the distance.

It was four miles. *Four motherfucking miles.* I froze midstretch. I looked up to catch both Jojo and Tim watching for my reaction. I know my mouth was an absolute perfect O when I shook my head. They nodded. My eyes filled with tears and laughter and disbelief as we all high-fived and headed back to our cars. Tim hugged me and pointed out that it was about time for me to sign up for my first 5K. *Me? Run a 5K? Who even am I?*

Chapter Seven

REMODELING TO RECONCILIATION

ONCE UPON A TIME, I WAS A RUNNER TRAINING FOR MY first half marathon with a few 5K and 10K completion medals hanging next to the mirror in my closet. I had ignored and maligned and hidden my offending breasts for almost a lifetime by this point. Now that I was being uncharacteristically and shockingly athletic, my breasts were again physical obstacles to my goals. I'd had to find an actual jog bra that fit, an outrageously difficult and expensive process, and even then they felt unwieldy and in my way when I just wanted to enjoy my pace with the wind at my back. And so, motivated by a desire to move without restriction, I began to revisit the idea of a breast reduction.

I'd wanted smaller breasts for many years, primarily because of the attention they brought me. My breasts brought me derision, adulation, lust, envy, embarrassment, clumsiness. Never grace. I wished for the option to take them the fuck off and put them in a bag some days. Athleticism never felt like an option for me when I was younger, outside of the supportive crucible of my boot camp family. Even dance became distant by early adulthood because girls built like me danced on poles, not on barres. That was just how it was. They defined where and how I belonged in all the spaces I moved through.

I had royally fucked them up even more by getting pregnant at sixteen. My lovely 36 C's rapidly ballooned in a way that was impossible to hide. Meanwhile I was masterfully denying and delaying confronting the reality of it. Fascinated by the way they defied physics, kind of in love with the eye-catching way they filled out new dresses in the fitting room at Macy's, lying with a hint of outrage at the suggestion my mother suddenly made in such a fitting room that I . . . I, virginal me, might be pregnant? Of course not! How could she? Followed by getting blasted on whatever I could concoct from my parents' liquor cabinet while dropping acid and smoking all the weed anyone would hand me while contemplating throwing myself down the stairs into the basement because I was a precocious reader, and I knew how they did these things back in the day.

Damn fetus was undaunted by my clumsy self-destructive attempts to thwart it. Eventually I had to beg for funds and try to navigate a way to obtain an abortion without alerting my parents. A friend connected me with her kindly young aunt who had promised to "help" if anyone ever needed that sort of help, as thanks to another young woman who had helped her once. This young woman checked me out of school, posing as my aunt, and drove me to a low-key ob-gyn who did abortions on the down low. When the doctor examined me, he declared that I was at least fifteen weeks along, and I would need a two-day procedure and another $400 to proceed. At which point the kindly friend's aunt fraudulently signed a bunch of forms and told me that she could *not* bring me back the next day and that I *had* to tell my mom. And you know the wildest thing?

The night before, at the dinner table, I'd been nervous. I knew my mom felt strongly about abortion, having been forced into a Florence Crittenton home herself because she got pregnant in 1968 and had friends who had been injured in back-alley abortions, so her parents wouldn't consider that route. She was on her second or third martini, and I concocted a "friend" who was going for an abortion, and I was curious if Mom knew what it was like. Tipsy Mom that night did *not* put two and two together and told me about how she'd heard it hurt. A lot.

When I got home from the half-finished procedure with a cervix full of seaweed (seriously, google it; it's a fascinating process that belies how boneheaded the medical establishment usually is about opening women's bodies), she wasn't home from work yet. I retreated to my room, assumed the classic 1980s teenager position of being on my belly on my bed, feet in the air, on the phone, strategizing with one of my few trusted friends about how I was going to tell her.

Suddenly the door popped open, and she looked in. "Hey, I made you some lime Jell-O. When you get off the phone, I need to talk to you."

I just nodded. As soon as she shut my door (she shut my door gently, a sign of respect that was not always present in that volatile time of our relationship), I told my friend, "I don't have to tell her. She knows. I don't know how. But she made me lime Jell-O. She knows."

And she did. At some time during the day, sober Mom had

recalled the tipsy Mom conversation the night before and put it together with my emphatic denials about my body changes in that fitting room a few weeks earlier, and she knew. And she didn't come in the house yelling. She came in the house, noted that I was safely in my room, respected my privacy, and made me fucking lime Jell-O. My favorite, typically reserved for the sickest of days and the worstest of news. And when I went and sat at the table with her, she stayed calm.

"It was you, wasn't it?" was all she said. I nodded. And then I had to explain that it wasn't over. That I'd played the denial game too long, that I was further along than expected, that I needed her to take me back the next day and to bring another $400, and also could she pay the friend's young aunt who quite frankly broke the law posing as my relative and guardian back another $300?

She called my stepdad and told him to stop at the ATM and that she'd explain later. She called my dad. I could tell she was shocked—and hurt. But she didn't yell, and that was scary. I was used to her raging. Her calm let me know this was really a big deal. The next morning we got there early, and as we sat on the bench outside the doors of the medical center, which hadn't even opened yet, she said she was relieved it wasn't a "clinic" and that we didn't have to deal with protesters. And we sat quietly breathing through a beautiful Atlanta spring morning, and I was so relieved she was there. I had no idea how much fear I'd been holding the day before, when she was not there, until her presence allowed me to let it go.

Afterward, even though they'd written me a note to stay out of school the next day, I just wanted to go back. I wanted it all to go back to how it was before. The safety of that intimacy with my mother when it was critically needed meant that I never again failed to trust her when the shit hit the fan, but most of the time the shit wasn't hitting the fan, and we ultimately both returned to our normal roles during the normal times. And in the months following, she couldn't resist a dig here and there. The one that always bit the deepest was the fact that I'd gone and "ruined" my breasts before my time.

I believed her. They'd swelled up dramatically during those fifteen weeks of pregnancy, and then all of a sudden their reason for existing disappeared, and they depleted—never back to their original size, though, but enough that their new heaviness and extra skin made them sag in a way that seemed abnormal for a teenager. In hindsight? As I sit here at fifty years old, I can see they were magnificent in every way, but on top of all the practical challenges they presented, they were also heavy, pendulous, attention-seeking sacks of shame.

Later, I grew up and had the money for a breast reduction, but the time was never right. When I began my initial foray into learning about breast reductions, my marriage was failing. I had attained an enviable position at a prestigious law firm, but I was disillusioned about what that actually meant in terms of my life. I had a 401(k), a generous business and business-casual wardrobe, sensible pumps for the courtroom, and a knack for writing that wowed the law firm partners but left me feeling empty. A clever turn of phrase in a bench brief or an insurance-coverage opinion only teases the soul of a writer; it doesn't feed it. Getting a breast reduction then felt undeserved, and selfish. I shelved the idea, kept dressing up the body I hated in shapewear and unforgiving mesh panels and metal framing, kept judging others who lived more freely, and walked through life prematurely embittered. I took my frustration out on my husband, and at times, I'm sad to say, on my child. There was a window when I could have had the surgery, with funds that came to me unexpectedly after my grandfather's death. But I couldn't look at myself naked in the mirror, and I could not imagine what that change would mean or how it would alter my path. Unable to meaningfully connect with my body, I poured the unexpected resources into something that, at the time, felt more noble.

I put the money into renovating our home. I gutted my home because I was not ready to gut my body. I told myself that if we got the house right, my husband might find happiness there, that I might find happiness there. That we could complete the outward picture of success where surely happiness lived for my son. As the renovation project wound down, as we prepared to move back in, there was an initial thrill in the novelty. We rented a bouncy house for the kids who came to the housewarming party. We didn't have enough furniture for the new space, and it felt decadent to stride over so many feet of perfectly polished and interlaced hardwoods, joining the old, the original, to the new in a way that was magical to me. We did a good job. It was and is a beautiful and thoughtfully designed home with only the whisper of the original modest bungalow we began renting when I was seven months pregnant. But part of the price of ignoring my inner pain was the splintering of my marriage. And so this beautiful house we made was also Clint's and my final joint venture.

Seven years later, after the revelations of boot camp, after my divorce, and my new love, and then my new marriage and a complete reordering of my life, my mother died. As Dave and I looked at all that I wanted to do at that point, I decided that I would not deny myself a breast reduction any longer. I'd stopped distance running after a blown disk in my lower back and was constantly frustrated by the way my breasts hindered my ability to move through the world as an active person. I dove into research mode. I've always been someone who wants to know *all* the things about everything, even scary stuff when it affects me directly.[1] One reason I picked the surgeon I chose out of the four I interviewed was that he did such a great job explaining his methods to me in detail. So even though I'm typically quite squeamish when it comes to *other* people and their blood, I was fascinated to learn exactly how my body would be transformed and how it would heal afterward. I was quite possibly one of the most prepared patients without any medical background my doctor had ever seen. When you research breast reductions (which almost always include a lift), a lot of the befores and afters you see involve additional procedures, so-called mommy makeovers. A typical mommy makeover includes some sort of breast surgery combined with a tummy tuck and liposuction.

It was obvious that getting rid of excess breast tissue would help my back, but by that point I'd regained quite a bit of weight, much of it in a floppy belly that made one surgeon I interviewed exclaim in surprise when I told her I'd only given birth to one child (it was an easy decision not to hire her). I'd become frustrated that no matter how much I focused on my core and abdominal exercises, my belly stubbornly refused to change. Even when I lost weight, I still had that flap. As I write this, I've learned how universal that body shape is for middle-aged women who are not peculiarly set up due to genetics or an extreme workout regimen, whether they've had children or not. But at the time, I didn't know any of that, I was fully invested in the

---

[1] I wrote about everything I was learning and feeling on RealSelf.com in a surgery blog under the username Newzandile. As the date got closer, I even created a YouTube channel on which I posted post-surgery updates until about seven months post-op (username Newshape2015).

myth of flat belly superiority. I felt a bit guilty even thinking about a tummy tuck, but I also longed for it. As I poured over other blog posts and surgery descriptions, I began to learn that there are valid reasons to get a tummy tuck that aren't necessarily aesthetic.

I'd gained sixty pounds while pregnant, and I'd had an internal backlash against the pressure to get rid of that baby weight. I felt I was being a better feminist by not focusing on that and by not wearing anything to bind my stomach after birth. I had no idea that women did that for health reasons and not just for vanity. I hated it that people kept asking my due date when Chase was toddling around already, but I didn't want to feel I was succumbing to the emotionally toxic advertising aimed at new mothers. In hindsight it makes me angry that no one educated me on what was actually a valid tool to help my body heal.

As I dug deeper and examined myself (feeling my abs mid crunch), I discovered I suffered from a condition called diastasis recti. Simply, my ab muscles had separated down the middle during pregnancy (as they must do in almost all pregnant women), and because of the extra weight I still carried after giving birth and my rejection of binding my stomach back together, the two sides had never reknitted themselves. This meant that each side of my abs was working alone, and I had about a three-inch separation down the middle. This meant my ab muscles were ineffective at supporting my spine and my breasts no matter how many crunches I did, and it left me at greater risk of developing a hernia.

Again, as I sit here now, I wish I could have felt that wanting a tummy tuck would have been valid regardless of the reason, but I carried shame around the fact that I had the power to change something that so many women feel they do not. In a way it felt like cheating (after having lived through the surgery and recovery, I'm here to tell you it isn't the easiest way, but endless exercising to achieve a specific look that is likely not possible nor even preferable isn't either). But the science of why it made sense appealed to me, so I shifted my focus from breast reduction to a "total mommy makeover" (ugh, I still cringe over the name of the procedure). I hired a personal trainer that summer to help me get in the best shape I could before surgery, and before long I had surgery scheduled for November 25, two days before Thanksgiving and just over five months after my mother's death. While I was super excited, I was also scared. I thought I was as prepared as I could be, but I was signing up, intentionally, to put my body through severe trauma in hopes that the outcome would be a net positive. There were absolutely no guarantees, and the informed-consent documents were long and frankly horrific.

The recovery was challenging. It was months before I could sleep in my own bed again, opting instead to sleep in a recliner. But the results were dramatic, and eight years later it is difficult for me, without seeing pictures, to recall what it was like living in my old form.

My feelings around plastic surgery are complex. My surgery had absolute health benefits that were real and welcome. The three-inch gap between my abdominal muscles was closed and permanently sutured together. While it was a long time before I was cleared to do ab exercises again, once I could, those muscles were finally able to work effectively to support my core and, coupled with the sixteen pounds removed from my chest in the breast reduction, I've lived largely free from back pain since surgery. When I think of the decades of my life spent being incapacitated by back pain, I'm overwhelmed by gratitude that I had the ability to have surgery. But the surgery also *drastically* changed my appearance. So much so that while I felt some shame about having the tummy tuck, that people would think I was being vain and somehow anti-feminist, ultimately I knew it would be obvious, so I decided to be open about it, and I've stayed that way.

Eight years later I've actually gained back all the weight that I lost preparing for surgery and during surgery, but I carry it differently. Surgically removed fat doesn't come back, but I do carry visceral fat in my upper abdomen, which means if I'm bloated or just super relaxed, I look a bit pregnant and like I'm carrying my uterus high. But I no longer have a tummy pooch. There's no loose jiggly fat around my midsection. I just look *solid*, which I don't mind. I do have a huge scar that wraps around to my back on both sides of my hips, but it's faded a lot everywhere except in the front middle. I don't bother trying to hide it. My surgeon placed it well, so it's covered by all but the most micro of panties or bikini bottoms. I like the way I look, but I hate the idea of someone, especially middle-aged women whose bodies are perfectly normal and lovely as they are, comparing themselves negatively to me and assuming I simply worked harder for it. I have worked hard for my health, and surgery was far from *easy*, but it is a path that can be toxic when it's hidden and others are made to feel they are deficient for not having what my body "achieved" through surgery.

The breast reduction also involved a lift. I'm not small now by any means. I really wanted to go down to a C cup, but the surgeon was clear that that would have been going too far, both for my health and because I wouldn't be proportional or happy with the results if he forced them that small. Ultimately I ended up in the DD to E range, depending on fluctuations in my weight and the vagaries of bra sizing between brands.

I can buy bras at places like Target and Walmart and Victoria's Secret without having to go to specialty stores or spend over one hundred dollars per bra. An even bigger win is that I actually don't have to wear bras anymore at all. My breasts are naturally perky now. They look more like ideal breasts than real breasts, but I love them so much. Overnight I went from, at best, not being repulsed by the sight of my naked breasts to being utterly delighted by them. I now know that my pendulous downward-pointing breasts were totally normal. They were not ugly. They were unwieldy and practically limiting at times. But they were not *wrong*. Knowing that, accepting that, and also loving their new look are all OK. I was enough before, and I believe I'd have eventually found my peace with them without surgery. But I'm also grateful for the gift of urgency that my mother gave me. And I appreciate a body part that caused so much pain for so long.

I would love a world where humans were celebrated in their natural form so that all of us could understand the range and variety of what natural humans look like. In this world we could know deeply, not just intellectually, that the range presented to us in popular culture is drastically skewed and does not encompass the vast majority of humanity. Then, with that depth of acceptance, choices to modify one's body could be made and shared and celebrated as empowerment to actualize your body in whatever way serves you best. Before surgery I didn't understand any of this, and I might have carried even more shame about having surgery had it not been for something that happened right before: my husband's surprise presurgical gift.

Chapter Eight

REVEALING TO RECONCILIATION

A COUPLE OF WEEKS PRIOR TO SURGERY, DAVE TOLD ME to pack for someplace hot. That was all he would say, and that was how I found myself standing thirty feet away from a ticket counter on a Thursday morning at the international terminal while he checked us both in. I followed him through security while he kept possession of both my passport and my boarding pass, asking each checkpoint person not to ruin the surprise. I stayed just behind him, reassuring them that this was all consensual and I wasn't being kidnapped. To a person, they all found this delightful, and he got a lot of props and high fives.

He'd gotten us there early, and we spent a few hours going from gate to gate, with stops for cocktails and snacks, while he faked me out over where we were headed. Finally we ended up at a departure gate showing Montego Bay as the destination, and he grinned and handed me my passport and boarding pass.

I was delighted. I've yet to meet a Caribbean destination I haven't enjoyed, after all. We landed and arranged a taxi to take us to Negril, about a ninety-minute drive over a very winding road, during which I was convinced we were going to take out a wayward goat, a family of chickens, or a child or two in their improbably pressed and blindingly white-shirted school uniforms. We made it without incident, and as we turned down a short side street to our hotel, I gasped. Just to our left was a sign: Hedonism II.

I gaped open mouthed at Dave: "You booked us at *Hedonism?*" He shook his head, confused. "No, what's that?" He gestured to the right, just across the street, to our actual destination: the Grand Lido Resort.

I started breathing again. He had no idea what my distress had been about, but I'd read about Hedonism years before. I remember looking at a brochure with my first husband and both of us wondering how anyone could be comfortable vacationing naked, especially since everyone pictured in the brochure looked like a bodybuilder or a bikini model. I told Dave about that memory, and we laughed about it and then walked through the rather grand (but also rather dated) open-air lobby of the Grand Lido.

When they showed us on a resort map where our room was situated, both of our eyes popped wide again. Just around the corner from our room, the next building over, was an area designated "clothing optional" on the map. Dave blushed and scrambled to assure me that he'd booked a package on Orbitz, had not researched the resort at all, and had no idea there was anything "clothing optional" on the menu.

We got settled in the room, which was not as grand as expected, and went exploring to find lunch. Over the next two days we discovered that the "Grand" Lido resort was well past its prime and fighting to survive. Most of the resort was far from full, and while the ocean and the beach were pretty, there wasn't a lot going on. The restaurants were passable but dull, and the beach and pool scenes were downright boring. They had an earnest if meager entertainment crew that tried to muster excitement for trivia games and cooking demonstrations, but most folks seemed to be more focused on their books and themselves than on socializing. It felt like the resort was trying to feed an audience that hadn't shown up. We also endured a time-share presentation that felt more than a little desperate, the elegance and opulence of the model suite they showed us doing more to highlight the shabbiness of the current facility than to elicit excitement about the future.

Our room looked out to a point, and the buildings were arranged so that we couldn't quite see over to the clothing-optional section. But as we enjoyed cocktails and got bored of staring at the water, we admitted, with the giddiness of preteens, that we were mighty curious to see what it was like over there. It was clothing "optional" right? They couldn't *make* us take our clothes off, so there'd surely be no harm in walking over. We could make it look like we were on our way somewhere else. They'd never have to know we were essentially peepers!

As we tittered, a paunchy older man with long white hair strode around that corner, completely nude and completely without a care. He looked like an aging rocker. He was with a woman who had adeptly rewrapped her sarong to cover her breasts. She appeared to indicate to him that they had left the clothing-optional section, but he honestly didn't seem to care, and he went on a few more steps before shrugging and turning back, presumably to grab some shorts. OK, now we had to check it out.

In hindsight I can't help but chuckle at our nerves. Our hearts were racing as we rounded that corner on the path to the proverbial forbidden garden. My worst fears were immediately realized as we almost ran into a nude woman who looked, I kid you not, like a twenty-first-century Bo Derek, all blonde braids and perfectly glowing tan and toned skin. Great, so the paunchy old dude was *not* the norm, and all the folks over here were going to make me feel like the dowdy middle-aged frump I really was.

To my surprise, she met my eyes, graced us with a radiant grin, and asked how we were, standing there as if talking to a gorgeous nude woman was something we did every day. I mean, I *have* done it, but only in illicit spaces like strip clubs. This, this was such a freaking wholesome environment (the shabbiness of the buildings aside). There were flowers blooming everywhere, lush grass, the pounding of the ocean, the sea breeze, and the sunshine leaving nothing to the imagination. She seemed to collect the rays and reflect them back on us as if it were the most natural thing in the world.

Her greeting was so unexpected—women like this didn't need to talk to people like us. I have no idea what we stammered in response.

"You should join us at the pool, I'll be right back!" she said. And then she was gone. Thoroughly flummoxed, wanting to flee but not wanting to look like idiots, we put our heads down and continued along the paved path.

The pool was off to our right but was mostly blocked by the

building that housed the pool bar. Once we got past that visual obstruction, we were amazed at the scene. The pool was hopping with people—in it and next to it and on the loungers. Most of the folks (as much as we could tell in our awkward attempts at glancing without actually looking) were much more like us and the paunchy old dude than the supermodel who had just greeted us. Some of them were dancing. There was great music playing and so much talking and laughing. There was no entertainment crew over here—these folks didn't need it. Some of them had noticed us and were smiling invitingly, but we picked up the pace.

I was thinking, *OK, this has given us some stuff to talk about, but right now I just want to get the hell OUT of here!* We'd really not thought this part through, though, assuming we could walk through the clothing-optional section and then circle around the building on the other side, just pass through. But as we got past the pool area, we realized, in horror, that it was a dead end. There was a picturesque gazebo overlooking the ocean before the fence that barred our escape (which was below low cliffs beyond the pool), so we hastily decided to pretend that that had been our destination all along.

As we stood in the gazebo gazing anywhere *but* at the pool, we noticed there were more naked people down on the rocky beach, and several hanging out around a huge doughnut-shaped float, breasts bobbing in the gentle waves, cocktails in hand. We assiduously studied flowers by the fence, suddenly fascinated by the local botany.

"We're going to have to walk back that way," I hissed. I knew my face was red.

"I know," he said. He was blushing, too, but also laughing at our ridiculous predicament. Here we were, two intelligent people in our forties acting like we'd never seen naked adults before. But in actuality we had never been in a socially nude situation with other adults. Most Americans haven't. Part of me was screaming that I wasn't supposed to see these parts of other people unless I was paying them, or they were perfectly airbrushed and art-directed for the sale of a product or for my own pornographic desires. It felt fundamentally indecent to think you could just stand around naked in the sunshine and talk about normal things.

We took a few deep breaths and resolved to get back to our room as fast as we could. We reminded each other we hadn't done anything wrong. It's not abnormal to take a walk around a resort where you've paid for a room, after all.

As we passed back by the pool, one woman in particular caught my eye and held it. She grinned impishly but not unkindly and invited us to the fun side of the resort. "C'mon over! It's so much better on this side. We don't bite, I promise!"

I grinned back at her despite myself, quickly cataloging the fact that, while she looked tan and healthy, she also was unabashed about her breasts not being firm, her belly having a roll in it, and her thighs being dimpled with cellulite. I felt a tiny thrill of rebellious joy that she wasn't bothered by things I had known for so long must, at all costs, stay covered on myself. I don't recall if or how we answered, but the rest of the walk back was a blur.

We started breathing again once we got to the room. "Do—do you want to go?" I asked.

He shook his head. I agreed. The pool seemed overwhelming, too much too fast. "What about the beach?" I asked. The beach wasn't crowded, and we could keep to ourselves. "I am totally not ready to be nude," I told him, "but maybe, maybe I might like to see what it's like to be topless? Outside?"

I was about to have surgery to remove the breasts that had defined me for so long. They'd bothered me and attracted attention and been a feature that almost everyone in my life had commented on in one way or another since I was thirteen. They'd betrayed me by sagging after my abortion, and they'd silenced my anti-breastfeeding mother by nourishing my son for his first year. They'd contributed to my aversion to all things sports and fitness, and then when I defied them and got fit anyway, they'd been a direct cause of injuries that had interrupted that process and robbed me of the will to pursue so many other active things.

I'd given up on golf and tennis because they were in the way. I was so frequently annoyed by them and had so often wished them gone, but now, as I stood here in this place where similarly imperfect women seemed to not mind their wayward, sagging, large, small, mismatched breasts, but walked around with them in the sunshine, I felt a bit of sadness that my breasts—my pain-in-the-ass, maligned-by-me, at-times-worshipped-by-others breasts—had never felt the sun before. Not once. All of a sudden it seemed the most natural thing in the world that I allow them this one thing before literally cutting them away from me.

I think Dave was surprised at this turn, and he said he wasn't ready to be nude, either, but he'd put on swim trunks and go with me if I really wanted. And so we put on our bathing suits. Mine was a tankini, my normal style, with a high-waisted bottom to hold in my tummy pooch and a separate top because my breasts were so large they always needed a different size than my bottoms. For once, though, I didn't feel that I had to put on a cover-up to protect the world from the fat rolls on my back, my chubby upper arms, or my chunky thighs that jiggled and rubbed together with every step.

That thrill of rebellion I'd felt when locking eyes with the woman at the pool had found root in me, and I strode out our patio door and toward the nude beach, conscious that my thighs were also getting more sun than usual. The clothing-optional beach was rocky, with a small cliff that kept it hidden from the resort at large. Once we'd wound our way around, we found a little area that was relatively private and not far enough down to catch the notice of the others who were around a bit of an outcrop.

The folks hanging out on the doughnut float could see us, though, and I noticed that they had glanced our way and were aware of us. Dave found a spot to sit, clearly uncomfortable. Hell, I was awkward and nervous too. But I'd made up my mind, and I wasn't leaving without doing what I'd set out to do. My breasts were like a terminally ill patient, and I'd heard their last wish and was hell-bent on granting it. I took a deep breath, faced the surf, and removed my top.

For an instant, my breath caught, I felt a sense of falling, and in the momentary panic I tried to rush forward to the welcoming shelter of the water. I had, however, not planned this part well. The shoreline was rocky, and the water was shallow farther out than I'd expected. I couldn't run forward without, at best, stubbing a toe, and at worst tripping and falling and looking not only half-naked, but half-naked and ridiculous.

I was acutely aware that the folks floating laconically, hanging on the side of the giant doughnut, could see me and were likely watching. I wanted to show Dave, who stayed up on the beach, wrestling with his own anxiety about this experiment, that I could be bold and brave, because if I could show him that, then maybe I could convince myself. So with deep but shuddering breaths, I kept my hands out by my sides, using my arms to balance as I tiptoed around the rocks, shuffle stepping through the small open stretches of sand to avoid sea urchins and the like. It took an eternity for the water to reach my knees, my hips, my belly, and then, at last, I gave myself the release of sinking down, allowing my pendulous breasts to hit the water, thinking they'd slide right out of sight.

I turned back to face Dave, and he waved, still looking uncomfortable but gamely showing his support. I'd also turned back because I'd just realized what unencumbered breasts do in salt water, and sinking out of sight wasn't on their agenda. My heavy, veiny breasts with their saucer-size areolas were not hiding. They were floating. Initially it was an odd sensation. I could see them, attached to me but stretching away from me, yet without weight, no pulling on my skin or my shoulders or my back. The skin underneath my breasts, that poor, always-stressed skin, always-sweaty skin, always-irritated skin, frequently poked by errant underwires and marked by rough elastic was . . . it, well, it was soothed. I mean, I've taken baths before, of course, but in a bath—at least the baths I'd had access to up until that point—you're seated, or partly reclined, and your breasts don't have room to rise up and away from your torso, much less to be lifted and swayed independently of your body by the rise and fall of the surf. They'd never had the opportunity to be *this* buoyant, this free, this wild.

I measured my breath to match the rhythm of the ocean. I dunked under, wet my hair, kept walking backward into deeper water, and then lifted my feet. I'm a champion floater. And even though floating on my back meant revealing it all to anyone who was looking down from the cliffside pool area or over from the doughnut float, I couldn't resist. And so I floated. The sun, the sea breeze, the salt water, the waves, it was all delicious. I felt overwhelmed with gratitude for this moment, and for these unwieldy, pain-in-the-ass breasts. I came upright again and marveled at their floating, their freedom, the sudden perkiness of nipples that rarely woke up because they were almost always under multiple layers of cloth. I gathered them back to me. I cradled them. I laughed at the absurdity of the depth of feeling this simple act was bringing me. Why had it taken me until the age of forty-two to experience this moment? Had my recently dead mother ever known this? Had my grandmother?

In a flash, a white-hot ember of rage took hold, and I began crying in earnest. I don't know for sure, but I'm guessing my mother and my grandmother had *not* known this. And why not? Why the fuck had my breasts been a source of pain rather than joy to me? Why had they made me a target to predators and a danger to civil society? There was absolutely nothing inherent in them, in me, that made it make any sense that the law and convention had draped them, and me, in so much shame. All while half the population walks anywhere they like topless, without a care in the world, with no appreciation of the gift of sunlight and sea air and ocean waves that their nipples enjoy anytime they like.

Dave, sitting topless back on the beach, was doing what he'd always done at any beach, and no one had ever questioned it. My rage was not at him specifically, but there was anger aimed at all the men who have thoughtlessly enjoyed this simple human delight and told a woman she could not, should not, enjoy the same. Or even just judged a woman for doing so. The absurdity of the shame placed on femme bodies becomes even more arbitrary when you see trans men suddenly free to go topless with the exact same nipples they had pre-top surgery simply because some fat has been removed, and for trans women to have to learn that, just as they want to excitedly open their tops to show their new growing or surgically enhanced breasts, they frequently cannot because they are in public. Again, exact same nipples, same skin around them, same human underneath.

Enjoying a tropical beach topless is a human right. It is *your* right. I urge you to claim it.

Dave called out to see if I wanted a drink. I did, and he said he'd be right back. While I was waiting for him, still bobbing in the surf, reveling in the fact that my breasts were enjoying this sojourn before they changed forever on a surgeon's table, the folks on the doughnut float called out to me. "Those look amazing!"

I spun around a bit, probably blushing. One of the women laughed. "I think he meant your tattoos, (I have several and the top half of my back is covered by a large and detailed piece with a forest scene). We'd love to see them! But what you have on the front is gorgeous too!"

She winked and I gave a nervous laugh. "C'mon over," she shouted. "We've got room!"

"I'll come over in a minute," I called back. "Just waiting for my drink!"

I knew Dave was anxious about all of this—titillated and curious, but also anxious. I figured that his coming back from the bar to find his newly topless wife no longer alone but in proximity to mixed company without him might be a bit jarring. But I was grateful for their friendliness. It didn't feel creepy in the slightest, and the vibe they gave off was playful, but not even in an overtly sexual way. Their compliments gave me heart, and I was close enough to see, even though their full bodies weren't out of the water, that they were all normal people. Not a supermodel among them, all of them likely middle age.

I waded partway back up to the beach to meet Dave for my drink, getting far enough out of the water that my breasts were again fully exposed and no longer floating, lying in their natural position on my torso. My anger had also sparked more courage, and I wasn't desperate to try to hide in the water again.

I relayed the invitation to Dave, but he was hesitant. He can be the life of the party when he knows everyone well, but in new settings he likes to hang back and observe, and this was hardly a normal new setting. After only a few minutes of discussion, he encouraged me to go ahead, and he'd be fine. I wasn't quite sure if he really knew he'd be fine or was simply hoping, but my curiosity to meet these unabashedly naked basking humans was too intense, so I kissed him and began wading, treading, and awkwardly swimming out to the float with my drink held above the water.

I don't recall anything specific about the conversation with that friendly, languorous bunch. I do recall laughter, their enthusiastic approval of my tattoos, their delight in hearing that this was the first time I'd let my magnificent breasts free, and the way they made me feel so quickly like I belonged among them. I do recall the word *magnificent* and feeling wonder that strangers were seeing my breasts—unadorned, unlifted, unlaced—and that they used the word *magnificent* to describe them, as if it were the most obvious descriptor in the world.

I didn't mention that I was getting ready to have surgery. I just hooked an arm over one edge of the float and in minutes was interwoven into their conversation and vibe as if I'd always been there. It was as if, being free from clothing simultaneously made them and, dare I think it, me free from social inhibition. Not social skill or respect. No one was doing anything sexual or making overtures. It was obvious by the playfulness and the eye contact and the body contact between some of the folks that there was a mix of couples—and maybe throuples and singles in the group. But the conversation was as wide ranging as it might be at any beach bar, perhaps more wide ranging. No one had to concern themselves with maintaining quite the same level of decorum one would if meeting while clothed, but no one was being wild and unhinged either.

I don't recall any conversation about what folks did for a living, or even where they lived. It was as if, unadorned with all the social signaling we do with our clothing and accessories, the reality that the most interesting features of our lives are rarely our jobs or our hometowns was just obvious. Without touchstones (brand names, clothing styles) with which to size someone up, when confronted with people in their raw human forms, their facial expressions, their voices, and the way they make eye contact become the primary ways to learn about someone. And those vulnerabilities invite you in and invite you to open yourself to sharing stories from your life that would not typically be cocktail-party fare.

I soaked it up, my breathing relaxing and becoming normal, my laughter genuine, until I reached the bottom of my cocktail. Not wanting to leave Dave alone on the beach any longer, I bid them farewell and said we might see them later, then made my way back to Dave.

Confidence boosted, a little tipsy, I agreed it was time to regroup after he said he wanted to head back to the room. I had to redon my bathing suit top before we rounded the corner, but I exalted in the short walk up to that point, still topless, and felt that stab of resentment and rage again briefly as I struggled to get the top back on over my wet skin.

That night, hyped up on this feeling of freedom, we went looking for a bit of entertainment and adventure and found nothing remotely interesting going on at the resort. We sipped more cocktails and wondered aloud about the place across the street, that place that was apparently so wild and free and hedonistic they claimed it right up front on the sign at the entrance: Hedonism II.

Loaded up with liquid courage, Dave finally stood up and said, "Hell, let's walk over there. Let's just see what it's all about."

And so we did, hearts racing even more than during our dead-end pool walk. We made it as far as the guard shack at the beginning of the drive into the portico area of Hedonism. Standing there, unsure of whether we would be allowed to just walk past it, a friendly dread-locked guy stuck his head out the window and gave us a gigantic and welcoming grin.

"How can I help?" he asked.

Feeling ridiculously shamefaced, we sidled over to him, puffing ourselves up like this was the most natural thing in the world. "What's the deal with this place? Is there any way we can check it out?" I asked.

The guard shack guy was fabulous and welcoming. Yes, we absolutely should check it out. In fact, our interest was not at all unusual, and they offered a pass program where couples not registered at the resort could pay for a day pass or a night pass for access to the entire resort for twelve hours (except for guest rooms).

Yes, it was all inclusive, and our pass would give us access to food and all the alcohol and entertainment. It was Rock Star Theme Night, in fact, and there'd be a DJ with a dance party on the main pool deck into the wee hours, with a high-energy entertainment crew livening things up further.

Yes, we could be clothed or naked everywhere but in the restaurant areas, where clothing was required, but if we went down to the nude beach and nude pool area, we would be *required* to get naked. That was a shock, but he reassured us that we absolutely didn't have to go there if we didn't want to, but that pool *was* the only one open after hours. It would be $150 for the two wristbands, and we'd have to leave our IDs at the front desk while we were on the property.

Unsure, I think, whether we were both on the same page and not wanting to be *that* vulnerable with the friendly ambassador, we said we'd think about it and scurried back to our room. To my surprise, given his apparent nerves at the beach earlier, Dave said he thought we should do it. His reasoning was impeccable. We could afford to burn $150, not that it wouldn't sting a bit, but it wouldn't kill us, and if we didn't do it, we'd always wonder what we were missing.

By the time we finally made it back across the street, getting a hearty thumbs-up from the guard shack guy as we passed on our way to the lobby, we were abuzz with anticipation, our eyes as wide as plates. I could not quite convince myself that someone wasn't going to jump out of the bushes at any moment, like some sort of labyrinthian troll, and say, "Aha! You are not welcome here! *You* don't belong here!" And yet no one stopped us.

When we stood at the registration counter and indicated we'd like a night pass, the attendant, while polite enough, was thoroughly bored by the request, like she didn't even realize how brave we were being. We had to fill out paperwork, and I don't remember any of it, but I'm sure it involved acknowledging the nature of the environment we were entering and affirming that we would not hold them responsible if we were traumatized by the sight of nudity or debauchery.

My first thought was that we should take advantage of the buffet and sop up some alcohol with food before we got ourselves in trouble, but we'd taken so long hemming and hawing and trying to decide what to wear that they were closing it down, so I grabbed bread and a small dessert, and we sat in the open-air dining area—acting like we totally belonged there—and took in the people and the sights around us.

The clientele, many of them in Rock Star Theme Night costumes, clearly were mostly our age or older, with folks who looked like they'd never partied to Def Leppard or Bon Jovi definitely in the minority. It was clear lots of folks knew each other, but there also seemed to be free-flowing conversation all around. I kept hearing people compliment each other in ways that made it clear they *didn't* know each other. It was just an intensely friendly and social environment in a way nightclubs never are in my experience.

We got more drinks and headed out to the main pool deck, where the dance party under the stars was getting underway. The sun was down, but it was still Jamaica, and it was hot. The entertainment crew was leading the way on the dance floor, encouraging folks to come out and start moving. They were gorgeous people who were also so engaging. Before long a beautiful, glistening, muscular Jamaican man had pulled me onto the floor, and I felt years of telling myself my dancing days were over melt away. Before we knew it, Dave and I were fully immersed, dancing with each other, with the professional dancers, with the other guests. Screaming with delight when a great song came on. Jumping and twirling and getting lost in the music in a way I thought I'd never know again. I felt the child's unrestrained connection with my own body, at one with every human heart within earshot of the beat. And so, not once upon a time, not someday, but now, I danced.

Somewhere approaching 2:00 a.m. we were flagging, our clothing, much more substantial than what almost everyone else was wearing, was heavy with sweat, constricting and uncomfortable. The main pool, right next to the dance party, looked enticing, but it was closed, and no one was allowed in.

We decided to wander a bit to see what the "nude" side looked like. We found our way down to the main beach and the dock. We rounded the water sports building and saw the infamous Hedonism II "Nude Beach" sign. Hand-painted on a piece of plywood and nailed to a tree, it simply says, "Nude Beach, No Clothing Beyond This Point."

There was no one out on the beach at that spot. No guard or attendant. There was nothing to stop us from walking past it with our clothes on, but what the hell? It was dark, we seemed to be alone, and we'd just spent a few hours in the company of people who didn't seem to care what people looked like. So we stopped in our tracks and removed every stitch of clothing, suddenly awkward and shy with each other.

"Let's walk closer to the water," I said, mindful of the windows of the rooms facing us. And so we wrapped our clothes up in bundles and made our way to the water's edge, delighting in how amazing the night air felt on our skin. We dropped our clothes on a beach chair and shuffled out into the water. It was magic—two humans naked and alone in the ocean. I felt so much gratitude for this moment, this unlikely moment that we wouldn't *ever* have planned from our comfortable life at home, this moment we'd stumbled into by accident.

We held each other, we laughed, we kissed. We wondered at the fact that there weren't any other people on the beach. I could see the pool bar, the side that faces the beach is a walk-up; the other side is a swim-up, accessible from within the nude pool. I could see there was a bartender on duty. Over the sound of the mild surf I could hear voices from that direction, and then some folks walked by, hand in hand, totally nude, and they headed up the steps toward the pool.

I looked at Dave and raised my eyebrows. *Do we dare?* He nodded. By this point we were reasonably sure that no one would point and laugh at us. And so we stepped back out of the relative safety and obscurity of the ocean, grabbed our clothes, and with a fortifying deep breath strode into the lights around the pool area.

Past the pool we could see what looked like a second pool that had more people in it. It was shaped like a clover, and we soon realized it was a hot tub, the largest I'd ever seen. We approached it steadily, not scurrying, acting as if we had every right to be there, and slowly walked down the steps into it, leaving our clothes on another nearby lounger. A few couples socialized in or on the edge of the tub, and others kept to themselves, clearly occupied with each other in various ways. We settled in on the bench and kept ourselves small, trying not to stare, trying to quietly talk, but both of us were acutely interested in everything happening around us.

My heart was racing. Being topless at the beach had been a big move, but I'd just walked, completely nude, under lights, with my belly hanging and my thighs jiggling, and my breasts hanging lower than they were "supposed" to, and these folks had all watched. No one had recoiled or made a face. A few people even smiled in our direction, but it wasn't the open atmosphere that it had been at the dance party or on the doughnut float. It certainly wasn't unwelcoming, either. It was just a 2:00 a.m. chill vibe.

I breathed into it. And then realized I really had to pee. I looked around and identified the location of the bathrooms. The thought of exiting the water again, my ass rising past eye level and drawing attention as I went, and having to walk around the tub to get to the bathroom was still scary, but I was certainly not going to be that person who pees in the hot tub. I girded myself and took the railing alongside the steps, forcing myself to breathe and walk slowly the entire way, ignoring the feeling of eyes on me, focusing on where I was stepping (I was barefoot, after all).

The path to the women's room was quite narrow and passed the men's room, so that a man coming back had to step aside and make room for me. He gave me a happy boyish grin as I passed. I nodded and gave a half smile back and made it to the safety of the women's room. Washing my hands, seeing myself naked in a public restroom in the mirror, was a shock, but in a way that made me smile and wink at myself.

I wiped away the smudged eye makeup, squared my shoulders, and made my way back. Standing by the increasingly crowded hot tub, naked and no longer afraid, I thought about this body I was in. I thought about this body that had done so much for me, and which had always been both too much and not enough for my happiness.

I had not been fair to this body. This body that had allowed me to dance. This body that had allowed me to swim. This body that had built my son from scratch and then nurtured and fed him. This body that had brought me back to myself at boot camp. This body that had been sexually assaulted and raped but had survived. This body that had held and shared pleasure beyond holding. I had been so unkind to this body when it had deserved nothing but my gratitude and my respect.

In fact, I was preparing to carve it up in just a few short weeks.

I walked slower. I stood off to the side of the hot tub, in full sight of everyone who cared to look my way, bathed in the moonlight and the lamplight, caressed by the breeze of the salt air, tickled by dripping water, glistening and starting to chill, and I closed my eyes and I apologized to my body for not loving it better. I thanked my body.

The changes I'm making are necessary for my health, I told it. You will be changed forever, but you have done well by me, and I'm sorry I never celebrated you without reservation. I'm sorry I inflated flaws that were just features. I'm sorry I hid you and carried shame that made you ache. I'm sorry I denied you for so long.

I felt tears prick my eyes, my body letting me know she heard me. For that moment, that night, she and I were one, and there was no more anger or disappointment between us. As I stepped back into the tub, I luxuriated in the warmth of the water, enveloping me like the beginning of a hug, a hug that Dave completed as I melted into his arms again, whole and content.

Chapter Nine

BECOMING BONNIE BODACIOUS, BUMPING & GRINDING TO BELONGING AGAIN

WITHIN A WEEK OF COMING HOME FROM THAT TRIP, I turned to Dave and told him that for my forty-third birthday I wanted to come to Hedonism II for a full week, and we were soon booked for October, eleven months after surgery.

Hedonism and the friendships we made there between 2015 and 2019 changed our lives immensely in many beautiful ways. Five years after first setting foot on the Hedonism II property, I was awarded the coveted Ms. Playful Pussycat sash and crown by our group leaders for best embodying the spirit of freedom and love and fun

that the group leaders worked hard to create through activities and
atmosphere. Given that the group by that point had swelled to about
250 people, it was quite an honor to be picked (and unexpected—I
was so shocked when they said my name I almost dropped my drink).
The story of how I went from timidly tiptoeing around the nude hot
tub at 2:00 a.m. in 2014 to winning an award for how dedicated I
was to living naked and out loud in 2019 was made possible in large
part by my burlesque journey.

By 2013 I had pretty much forgotten the joy of dance outside of
alcohol-fueled clubbing. I was clearly fat. Even after multiple boot
camps and feeling stronger and more capable in my body, I was certain no one wanted to see me dancing. It was my fate. My mother
and her sister, born to my petite size 4–6 grandmother, were both
fat through most of their lives, and they both constantly complained
about or blamed their weight and their appearance for all the things
they couldn't do, or that it would not be seemly to do.

I was well aware that fat women didn't dance. Not with abandon,
and certainly not on stage. But I missed performing and was delighted
to discover a community theater out in the burbs near our house
after a client invited me to see him and his daughter in a play there.

Inspired, I signed up for the next audition they had. After not
being on stage in any capacity since college, I landed the role of Linda
Loman in *Death of a Salesman*. I did alright, and I stuck around,
finding an unexpected theater family in my late thirties. It was a
mixed blessing. As much as I thrilled at connecting with a truth
about myself I'd repressed for a long time, there aren't many roles
like Linda. I was a middle-aged fat woman who wanted so badly
to play Blanche DuBois but instead ended up as the flower seller. I

was good-natured about it. This was prior to my mother's death and surgery. I kept plugging away with auditions and plays. I kept being resigned to being fat. To Spanx. To sensible clothing that highlighted my cleavage in a modest way while disguising my stomach and ass.

Dancing for an audience felt like a dream I'd once had as a character, certainly not a realistic aspiration for myself. Then, in 2016, post-surgery, with two full vacations to Hedonism II behind us, we got invited to a surprise birthday party in Chicago, and everything changed for me yet again.

We flew up on Friday, and the party was Saturday. We decided to stay in Lincoln Park for the hell of it, and as we were driving along the waterfront, I opened up *Time Out Chicago* and opined that we should find something interesting to do in the city on our free Friday night, when no one knew we were there.

At the time we were enthralled, as much of the world was, with *Game of Thrones*. And so, when I saw that the improbably named Gorilla Tango Theatre was the venue for a production of *Game of Thongs, a Game of Thrones Burlesque*, I was immediately curious. We headed to Boystown, bought tickets at the box office of what was clearly a dive theater, and then wandered down the street to a bar that offered artisanal cocktails, wondering aloud what burlesque even was. I knew it had something to do with striptease, but having only ever experienced strip clubs, I wasn't clear how *Game of Thrones* was going to fit in.

As a child I'd watched *The Benny Hill Show* with my granddaddy religiously every summer, and I thought it might be like that, a bit of scandal and playfulness but probably conceived by and run by the male gaze. We were pleasantly tipsy when we took our seats high up in the audience—far from the stage but then so aware of all the people filling the seats below us, who all seemed like normal, interesting, quirky folks. Certainly not a bunch of weirdos with a strange fat-dancing fetish.

The show began. It was all women. No men were emceeing or directing the action in any way. Women played the male roles in a caricature way that was incredibly funny and empowering. The show was scripted, and in every scene, every character somehow—through comedy and sometimes dance and sometimes choreographed "fighting"—ended up wearing nothing but a thong and pasties. But more shockingly, they also brought their bellies, and their thighs, and their cellulite to the party. They made no apparent effort to cloak these characteristics or to hide them. They jiggled and offered no apology. The breasts were everywhere. Small peach pits budding from flat chests to pendulous sacks of opulent flesh that swayed back and forth hypnotically, pasties pointed brazenly at the floor, flopping up when the person carrying them bent backward so that the rhinestones sparkled and caught the light and did nothing to hide that these were very much not magazine-approved breasts but real honest-to-goddess breasts that did what they fucking pleased when not imprisoned in spandex and wire.

I found myself holding my breath. Did anyone else see? That these women were breaking the rules? What were they doing on this stage with an audience of normal people who paid real money to see them? But then I'd laugh, because they were fucking hilarious. And when I laughed, I'd breathe again and notice that the audience was with me. They were laughing, too, because it was hilarious—the script and the acting and the pratfalls. Not because it was funny that these women were pretending to be something they weren't. The audience was fucking rooting for them. They could not fail because they brought the audience along in the most glorious FUCK YOU to the patriarchy and to fantasy fiction and to body policing.

When the show was over, I was gasping, trying to catch up with all the breaths I'd held while my heart had raced. I gazed at the women in the cast during curtain call with nothing but undying admiration and love. It was more than that. It was adoration, and adulation, and surprise, and awakening. I heard Dave softly say, "Oh fuck . . ."

I realized tears were running down my face and that he was staring at me. He looked like a man on a precipice who knew there was no turning back. "What?" I asked.

"You're going to do this, aren't you?" he said.

And in that moment I knew that I would.

Earlier that summer a lawyer I had befriended at the annual family law conference had asked me to come to Alchemy with her. Alchemy is a regional Burning Man event that had been happening in Georgia in October for several years, and she was an experienced burner. I'd kept telling her no, but as the unexpected gift of that first burlesque show kept percolating in my heart, I remembered that, just two years earlier, I'd promised to get out of my comfort zone with intention, to create opportunities to discover new adventures and to be open to the ones I didn't expect. I realized I was saying no because it felt like something a woman my age wasn't supposed to do, at least not so close to home, which was clearly absurd. And so, with only a couple of weeks' notice, I told Suzy I'd go with her, and thus began my introduction into the world of Burning Man via Alchemy.

Burners embrace and embody a set of principles, originally ten and now eleven—the eleventh being consent—because even intentional utopian temporary communities have to reckon with and address our rape culture. I learned so much in those few short days about the power of intentionality when we seek to understand the purpose and impact of our own behavior. The principles of radical inclusion, radical self-expression, and immediacy connected me to myself more deeply during that weekend under an absolutely magical moon, ethereal in the blowing dust and scudding clouds that reminded me of my connection to the earth.

I found myself wandering on my own, but not really alone, midday Saturday, soaking up the freedom and peace and curiosity all around me.

I followed the smell of the amazing grilled cheese bar hosted by the Wherehouse Camp, only to stand in line and make friends with all of us enveloped in the mouthwatering prospect of custom grilled cheese. In the midst of which, a long-lost friend literally materialized out of thin air when she blocked the sun and became haloed by it as my eyes adjusted. When I recognized her, I cried happy tears, feeling found and finder all at once. That totally happenstance connection led to the opening of a glittery door that is the door I didn't know I was waiting for but which was clearly waiting for me.

She was a friend from high school. We'd first met when we were thirteen and had spent a lot of time on stage together in the drama club. Our senior year she scored the role of Auntie Mame. I was jealous but also grateful to get cast as her best friend, Vera, and we freaking *killed* it. We'd run into each other during the college years, our circles overlapping somewhat, and we'd connected on Facebook, but she wasn't active there. When we got over our initial excitement about finding each other at Alchemy, I asked why she wasn't more active on her profile, and she blithely said it was because she was now a burlesque performer, and she spent most of her time being active on her performer profile.

My mouth opened wide with surprise. This was too unexpected and too delightful to believe! It had been less than a month since I'd become aware of the existence of this art form, and here was a trusted friend who was fully involved! Her boyfriend (who was with her) pointed out that she was not just a performer, but an award-winning one, and that she was also a teacher at the Atlanta School of Burlesque.

"There's a school?" I cried.

She grinned at me. "You should come to a show!"

I couldn't believe that this was falling in my lap like this. Less than two weeks later we went to a party at the Atlanta School of Burlesque. It was part Halloween party, part show (they were doing improv burlesque to karaoke), and part open house to celebrate their new building, a renovated old Victorian house painted top to bottom in turquoise blue with a mural of powerful women dominating one whole side, less than a block from the heart of East Atlanta Village, a hip part of town. I spent the party absorbing the personalities and costumes and conversation like I'd been dying of thirst and had stumbled into an oasis of sweet water.

In addition to housing the school, the building was also the home studio for their performance troupe: the Candybox Revue, of which my friend, stage name Lola LeSoleil, was a founding member. A few weeks after that I was sitting at a VIP table, watching my first Candybox Revue main stage show at Smith's Olde Bar.

We bought raffle tickets but didn't win. At the end of the show, Lola approached with a piece of paper. Her boyfriend had won a free six-class pass to the school, which he wasn't going to use and which Lola didn't need. Would I be interested?

I squealed with delight and literally jumped out of my seat to hug her. The way I'd finally said yes to Alchemy, almost last minute, and then found Lola, and then said yes to the party and the show, and then to have her offer me a free class starting just a week later seemed like the universe was screaming for me to follow this path. I want very much to believe that my mother found peace with her own body in the release of death, and that she set out these stepping stones for me to make sure I'd find my way to loving my body without having to die first. The beauty of saying yes to things that you once thought were not options for you is that it invariably leads to vistas you cannot imagine are yours to enjoy. But they are.

I took that class, and I performed in the school recital a few months later, trembling with fear about dancing in public and struggling to apply false eyelashes when I'd never worn them before. I have come a long way since that first show. Burlesque has taught me that I'm capable of more than I ever thought possible. Through burlesque I've learned that my self-imposed limitations were illusions, and I've gone far beyond just loving myself passively. Through burlesque I've learned the gift of loving myself out loud and hopefully inspiring others to do the same.

If you're anything like me, you have had that moment where you've said to someone, and meant it, that you "loved" them but weren't "in love" with them. This is a distinction that is in part a product of the Disneyfication of our expectations around romance. But I do think there is a kind of distinction. When we love someone, oftentimes we love them because it's expected, because there's a relationship that already existed, outside our scope of choice about the matter, and because the other person has fulfilled the basic requirements to maintain that relationship, and because we appreciate what they've done for us and feel a sense of obligation, often familial, to care for them in return.

This may be the way we feel love toward parents and other older family members, or siblings, or cousins. When we are "in love" with someone, the existence of a preexisting relationship is immaterial. The ties of familial obligation may or may not be present, but regardless of the existence of any other basis to maintain a relationship with that person, we *delight* in them. Their presence gladdens our heart and tickles our senses.

This is true in all kinds of relationships, not just those that may support sexual connection. I remember falling in love with my son in the hours after his birth. That first moment when it was just he and I, when the nurses were gone. His father was snoring on the armchair next to my bed, and the lights were low so we could sleep. He was swaddled next to me on the narrow railed hospital bed, and we just gazed into each other's eyes, consumed with joy at each other's presence.

Well, at least I was consumed with joy. His eyes were too young to perceive me clearly, in all likelihood, but still. I have had moments with each of my parents and older relatives where I experience that sense of falling, that delight in their idiosyncrasies, in their humor, in seeing their face break into a smile or a laugh, or in recognizing a piece of myself in their vulnerability. That feeling that your delight in the other's existence is its own reason to be close to them. It was in the mirrors of the burlesque school, in the camaraderie of troupe life, in the forge of the roar of an appreciative audience, and in the silence of an audience enthralled, that I fell in love with my body and myself.

When I first began classes, I was excited but also nervous. I was overwhelmingly anxious to do burlesque "correctly." I couldn't wait to start, but I was also terrified. It made it a bit easier to dress for some sort of role when I showed up for the first night of class. I unironically ordered a leotard, tights, gauzy wrap skirt, and leg warmers and arrived looking like I belonged on the set of my favorite eighties TV show, *Fame*.

The first class I took was Burlesque Level 1 with Roula Roulette. The youngest of the three owners of the school and leaders of the troupe (along with Ursula Undress and Talloolah Love), Roula has made teaching beginning burlesque a ministry. Her students in the years since I began have coined the term "Titty Church" to describe any class Roula teaches, because she takes you on a spiritual and soulful journey in all her classes, but especially with wide-eyed beginners, no matter their age or shape or experience level. It's never just about the bumping and grinding, learning to do a perky princess walk or a sultry drag step. Roula begins by connecting you to your body, all of it. The bits you like the least are not tolerated, but celebrated.

It's scary, it's awkward, and there's lots of floor staring in the beginning. But her enthusiasm and joy in her own ample and vivacious and sexy flesh is contagious. The first time she tells you to stop apologizing for taking up space, the first time she gets you to say it out loud, and then shout it in unison, it feels like the most obvious thing in the world.

It was standing in Roula's class, accepting her challenge to look myself in the eyes in the studio mirrors, that I recognized how much of my behavior to that point had been an apology to the world for existing in shapes and sounds and movement that were not approved by some unseen tribunal. Even in the socially nude spaces I'd grown to love in the year before discovering burlesque, I had still shrunk myself at times, still told myself it was enough to be there, that I shouldn't be too loud about it. And that was and is Roula's gift to me and to every student who screws up the courage to walk into her class and give themselves to the experience she offers. That is the foundation of authentic burlesque. Dance steps are a storytelling medium. Believing that the story is worth telling must come first.

Six years since my first appearance at an Atlanta School of Burlesque recital, I am certain that my presence on stage is welcome, that the audience is worthy of what I'm offering, and that I am worthy of their attention and admiration. While I love my body post-surgery, I've gained back every pound that was removed, and I'm a plus-size burlesque performer.

My ass is large, my thighs jiggle and dimple and rub together, my upper arms shake and swing, body harnesses get lost a bit in the bra rolls on my back. Sometimes my ankles swell, and I have to be mindful of that when I choose performance shoes. But I am also fucking magnificent. I'm desirable and sexy. When I deliberately make my body shake and jiggle on stage, the audience responds with roars of appreciation (and frequently with raining cash).

So much of burlesque is attitude of movement. Fear is contagious, and I followed the same arc most performers follow. When you begin, you are certain that the audience will be bored if you stop moving, so you don't. You fill every beat with a shimmy or a shake or a step ball change or a twirl. You lean on props, fans, boas, gloves to hold your audience enthralled. But, gradually, the more you perform, the more you see more seasoned performers, the more you realize that so much of good burlesque is in how you claim your power on stage. Some of the most arresting performers in the world are masters of being still, of holding the audience's gaze and communicating that their mere presence, the simplest reveal, is a gift of immeasurable value, and that they *know* their value, and that the audience is damn lucky to see them.

This kind of confidence is not at all related to whether their body is "commercially acceptable"—that is, thin and white with big perky boobs. I have seen performers of all shapes and races hold an audience completely rapt with stillness, with anticipation, with good face, with a masterful eye-fucking. And I've seen performers with commercially acceptable bodies fall painfully flat, their fear infecting everyone in sight and leaving the audience squirming and uncomfortable. The "it" factor is entirely internal.

Here I was with my surgically perfect breasts, suddenly realizing that knowing a particular body part is appealing is not enough to carry a performance. I mean, my breasts are magnificent, but if I carry them and share them in such a way that the audience feels as though I'm asking their permission to exist, I will get nothing but polite applause. I learned this painful lesson in one of my first club shows.

There are different types of burlesque shows. Many of our regularly produced shows are very theatrical in nature, with highly choreographed narrative-style acts. Club shows are not that. Club shows tend to happen at clubs, bars with dance floors. That is where burlesque and drag often meet. Rather than a theater setting with a seated audience, club shows may have a stage, but the audience is *not* seated; rather they're standing shoulder to shoulder right up to the edge of the stage. They may have just been dancing themselves, reorienting their attention to the stage because the emcee or DJ asked them to, but they are active participants in whatever is about to happen, not passive spectators.

While they are not the same as strip shows, club shows follow the expectations of strip clubs and drag shows more than they do theatrical burlesque shows. Numbers may be loosely choreographed, but not too tightly, because the audience is expecting your attention, your direct attention. Performers may consent to body tipping, but in my experience performers who don't want to be body tipped (which doesn't typically happen in a traditional burlesque show, where tips are thrown from a distance or collected in a bucket) don't tend to gravitate to club shows.

In a club show the energy is intense. You are inviting the audience to collaborate with you. You may invite them to touch you. You may ask to touch them. It is not at all unusual to leave the stage altogether to move among the crowd. You move to the music and the mood in the moment. You make eye contact. You invite, you tease, you torment. You share yourself in a much more direct way than you do with a theatrical stage, where you're elevated and separated by lights and seating. It's intoxicating and exciting and completely electric. You feel their hunger, their delight, and their scorn full on, without any concession to manners.

Club shows are scary for that reason. There's a wildness to that environment, a grittiness and intensity that can hurt. In general, burlesque audiences are a delight. There is a dialogue loop of supportive enthusiasm between the stage and the crowd, both sides rooting for each other's success and extolling each other's fabulousness.

At club shows that loop is less certain, and it was at a club show that I first experienced open rejection while on stage. It was one of my first club shows, when I was still unsure of myself, and on a weekend when another event had drawn many of the regulars, so the crowd was unusually sparse.

The performer who went before me was vastly more experienced. She was a bit chaotic, but she was hella engaging, and the few people present ate it up. It was a hard act to follow, but I'd come up with what I thought was a cute concept. A little cotton dress with rhinestoned rain "drops," an umbrella, then a double reveal, first to a blue rhinestone G-string and matching pasties, but then a surprise reveal to flesh-colored nipple rhinestoned pasties and a pair of flesh-colored thin panties rhinestoned to look like a vulva with a prominent clitoris. A bit of false nudity as a bonus in a space where nudity was not allowed in our state.

The music was LOUD and thumping. I can't recall the song now. In a club show you don't always have control over your music, but I'd gotten down to that reveal. I'd done some floor work and was striding out onto the small catwalk at the front of the stage, feeling I'd *earned* some body tips. I see a woman (it was a lesbian bar) standing off to the side of the catwalk with cash in hand. There is no reason to be standing by the stage during a show with cash in hand except to tip. The bar is on the far side of the room. She had a single folded longways, exactly how most people opt to present it to slide into the strap of your panty (or whatever other straps you might be sporting). I made eye contact, and she did not look away. I gyrated in her direction, and as I reached the point closest to her, I helpfully lifted the strap at my hip, offering her a home for that dollar bill. Without breaking eye contact, she put it back in her pocket.

Time stopped.

I'm sure my gyrations hiccuped as I tried to compute what had happened. Should I just head straight for the dressing room? I'd been a performer for much of my childhood, and by that point, even before I'd stumbled into burlesque, I'd been a community theater actor. I knew better. The show literally had to go on. Most of the audience was most definitely unaware of this exchange. This show had been advertised through my troupe, and I owed them the professionalism of finishing my set. I comprehended that all in a split second. It took everything I had to flip my head away from her, this coldhearted demon woman, and not allow the sting to show.

Afterward, the producer hastened to reassure me that the crowd was weird that night, that the energy was different because it was so empty, that I'd done a beautiful job, and that there was nothing I should have done differently. I greatly appreciated that kindness, although part of me wished they hadn't noticed I'd needed it. But I took the pep talk from her and from everyone backstage, even from the performer who had clearly outshined me with her experience and flexibility (she'd done a split against the wall in the set before mine, for crying out loud), and I completed my second set with a bit more armor around my heart but still bumping and grinding.

I fulfilled my obligation to my troupe and the producer and then I went home and cried. I had to dig a bit to find the courage to sign up for another club show, but I knew that when the energy was right, it was magic, and I decided that, at the very least, I deserved to have my last club show be something other than that awful night. In truth, I went on to do several more club shows, all of them better than that night, all of them affirming and energizing as club shows *should* be. I survived the rejection of a patron. I rose to slay again, and I've enjoyed the sensation of being body tipped. I've felt my power in commanding the devoted attention of club fans who clamored to buy my drinks and to dance near me at the after-party. And to enjoy all that in my forties? Well, I'm not going to lie. It was fucking sublime.

My stage name is Bonnie Bodacious. I started casting about for a burly name days before I performed in my first group number at a recital for the Atlanta School of Burlesque. It suddenly dawned on me that I'd be part of a burlesque show and that I didn't have a stage name, that my actual legal name would be announced, perhaps even printed on a program. I was still a practicing lawyer at the time (albeit part time), and was very much a high school marching band mom at a school in the suburbs.

In preparation for that first recital show, I had gotten my hair colored a very punk rock fire-engine red. I've always looked good in red, and I *loved* my new color. It radiated the enthusiasm for life that I was claiming with both hands. I knew I would take more classes, and I knew I would be in more shows. I suspected that at some point I might even start stripping and performing solo. It seemed a long way off still (and I hastened to assure the friends I invited to that first recital that I wasn't stripping, which belied the anxiety I had in the early days about crossing that threshold), but I had never been one to do things half-assed, so part of me knew I was going to need a stage name sooner or later. Initially I thought it would be Red

Dawn. I hadn't actually seen that film (or didn't recall the details if I had), but I had the feeling that it was a good name for a strong independent character who didn't give a fuck as she claimed her place in a dystopian postapocalyptic world. I saw myself as a redheaded *Tank Girl* character.

For weeks I went to and from classes, absorbing all the burlesque content I could find and looking for act and costume ideas that would manifest that persona to the world. But Red Dawn, she'd probably be strong, athletic, tough, and sinewy. She'd have punk lyrics memorized and punk-style tattoos on her arms and legs. She'd probably have a lot of piercings and would be funny but in a dark, sardonic way and would mostly be a loner.

None of that felt like me. It felt like a character I'd enjoy playing for a specific show, but not someone I could seamlessly become at event after event, show after show, because she was so far removed from me in reality. Not to mention, as much as I loved that red color, and it has continued to be my signature hair color now for six years, including it in my name would make me uncomfortably wedded to a particular look. What if I wanted to be someone else for an act, a show, a season? I'd have to keep the red or it wouldn't make sense.

After pouring over lists of burlesque and Roller Derby names, while I was listening to music on my way to class at the studio sometime after that first recital, the name Bonnie Bodacious popped into my head. I've always adored alliteration anyway, and Bonnie was my first dog, and I have Irish ancestors. And Bodacious? Well, that word summed up everything I was trying to be and how I wanted to live, now that I was armed with the painful knowledge that my brain might turn on me and that my only opportunity to live bodaciously was to do it now.

After class that day, I lurked in a corner at the studio, registering the name on the two lists that were maintained at the time, setting up a Gmail account (someone already had the obvious one but I snagged thebodaciousbonnie), and creating a Facebook profile and an Instagram account for Bonnie. By the time I got back in my car, Bonnie had officially been created, and I've never stopped loving the name. As much as I thought I wanted my persona to be tough and sexy and serious, in reality Bonnie is very much still me. Yes, I can be tough. I was a litigator, after all, but being tough involves putting on armor, which is an act at odds with the naked vulnerability that burlesque asks of me. At times Bonnie is a femme fatale, but in truth I feel most connected to the audience and the community as Bonnie when I am clowning or being vulnerable.

The clowning caught me by surprise. I had never seen myself as a clown, but my original signature act has always actually been a clown act. I just didn't realize it until I'd done it several times and kept changing it. I added googly eyes to my ostrich boa and eventually began doing clown makeup to match the costume (which is Victorian in style but in bold black and white stripes with red accents, somewhat harlequinesque). Now I fully embrace that act as a clown act, and recognizing it for what it is and leaning into it has made it much stronger.

One of the last times I did that act, at a fashion show and fundraiser for queer Black fashion designers, there were two young women in the audience who were obsessed with clowns, and they couldn't wait to meet me after the show. I still had my clown makeup on, so I stayed in character by only mime talking to them from a distance. One of my beloved troupe mates, Vixie Todd, has always been our resident troupe clown, and when she saw the changes I'd made, she grinned at me and said she'd always known I was a clown at heart. And that is absolutely true. I love making people laugh and poking fun at myself. I love the comedy in caricature, in taking a few qualities or mannerisms and exaggerating them till they veer *just* into absurdity but are still completely familiar.

I am a storyteller. Burlesque is, for me, primarily a storytelling medium. Most of my acts involve movement to music, but I once saw a performer from another troupe do spoken word while stripping, and it was absolutely mesmerizing. She recited a poem, poetry slam–style, accenting the stanzas with movement and striptease. At the time I hadn't even stripped for the first time yet but the act stuck in my head and informed my later decision to write the piece that really sparked the idea to write this book.

I didn't cross the stripping threshold till the spring of 2018. The Candybox Revue provided entertainment at Frolicon, an annual geek and kink convention that happens every year in Atlanta. I'd never heard of Frolicon before I was invited to join the troupe in February of 2018, but as a new troupe member, I wanted to help in all the ways I could. On Friday night of the convention one of our troupe leaders was coproducing a big stage show that I had volunteered to kitten.

A stage kitten is a burlesque stagehand. It is the stage kitten's job to set up each act (that is, to place a chair or props per the performer's instructions). It is the stage kitten's job to clean up after each act (to pick up the "stripper droppings" strewn about the stage and sometimes tossed into the audience and to make sure they are safely returned to the performer backstage). This may involve nothing more than picking up a dress and a bra, or it may involve sweeping up glitter or confetti or cookie crumbs or feathers or removing a tarp or actual set pieces or furniture. It may involve interacting with audience members to retrieve items that intentionally or otherwise found their way outside the boundary of the stage. And being a stage kitten also always involves looking sexy/adorable/cheeky/funny and interacting with the audience and with the emcee (or femmcee, as the case may be) to buy time for performers to get ready or to deal with unexpected hiccups backstage. In short, stage kittens are incredibly important and visible.

Most performers start off doing as much stage kittening as they can, because it gets them free admission to shows, a cut of the door, and maybe the tips, depending on the producer and show structure. It offers the opportunity to interact with performers, producers, and emcees, and gets them experience with audiences. There is a lot of bending over to pick things up in the most suggestive way possible, while making eye contact with the audience to let them know you know that they know that you're showing your ass on purpose.

It's good fun and it's an art. The best kittens know how to keep the show flowing without taking too much time or attention between acts. The best kittens have excellent comic timing and love the spotlight, because ultimately, by the end of the show, the audience has actually seen more of the kitten than they have of anyone else in the cast. A great kitten can roll with the punches when things go awry. They rarely speak but may be called on to do so in a pinch, to riff with the emcee to buy time or to encourage audience members to participate in raffles. When I started, *stage kitten* was the term almost always used. Now masculine-presenting stage kittens sometimes choose to be called stage panthers, and the term *prop tart* is becoming more common as the community strives to be more inclusive of gender nonconforming members.

The show I was kittening at Frolicon 2018 was called *Undressed to Thrill* and was produced by Ursula Undress and Fritz Krieg. Ursula was one of the founders of the Candybox Revue and the Atlanta School of Burlesque and their home, Metropolitan Studios. She was also one of my teachers and mentors. She epitomizes cool and effortless sexiness and confidence. She has the classic beauty of old Hollywood and has been doing burlesque long enough that the movements and stage presence are simply part of who she is. She's also an incredible choreographer.

I learned my love of Bob Fosse's signature style from Ursula. It wasn't until just before class one evening, when the other students hadn't come in yet and she told me I had excellent stage presence and she hoped she'd see me solo soon, that I seriously thought I was ready to throw my hat in the ring as more than a student in group numbers. So when she said she needed kittens for the show at Frolicon, I leaped at the opportunity. I'd kittened some small shows prior to that, but the Frolicon stage was big—big enough for two kittens—and I was joined by Sunshine Divine, because it was definitely a two-person job. Ursula was also responsible, with her partner and fellow troupe mate Oliver Gentleman, for coordinating burlesque karaoke the Saturday night of the convention.

Burlesque karaoke is an improv event. It's a karaoke party, kind of like any other, except that folks who sign up to sing get paired with a burlesque performer who shows up on stage in a random costume. The burlesquer has no idea to what song they are performing until the singer starts singing.

Up to this point, I'd not yet done a solo number, nor had I stripped on stage. I had a lot of ideas, and I had commissioned my first full burlesque costume for what later became my first signature act, but to that point I had performed only in group choreography, which could be raunchy but which did not actually involve striptease. I was taking as many classes as I could, but the idea of choreographing a number was overwhelming.

Initially, when Ursula asked me if I could help out with burlesque karaoke, I'd responded that I could be the stage kitten again. I'll never forget Ursula's text response. "Nope, you're strippin." I remember staring at the text, my heart quickening. I'd attended burlesque karaoke. I knew it was improv, that there was no need to choreograph anything. Comedy and absurdity were encouraged. I didn't have to take it seriously. It was actually probably the best way for me to cross that threshold, and I'm grateful that Ursula nudged me across that line. I didn't want to let her down, and I figured, *Hey, it's a convention on a Saturday night. How many people will actually show up? Much less, sober?*

And so, after handling my kittening duties Friday quite professionally, and enjoying the convention's classes and sights and vendor hall on Saturday, all while staying mostly sober, I retired to our suite to get ready to take the stage. I'd been told to bring three costumes and that I'd definitely use at least two of them, with the third in case the party was going well.

Almost five years later, I don't recall if I used two or three costumes. I just recall the first one. Kisa von Teasa, an experienced performer from Knoxville and a leader in a Knoxville-based troupe, was in town. They are bosom buddies with another of the Candybox

Revue's founders, Talloolah Love, and had been one of the headliners of Ursula's Friday-night show.

I was in awe of them. They were a bit younger than me but, like Ursula and Talloolah, they had been doing this long enough that they exuded complete confidence. They love improv and had jumped at the chance to do burlesque karaoke. I don't know who did the lineup, but they were before me in the first act, and I nervously struggled to get into my first costume. Although I don't recall specifics, I do remember the usual challenges of professional fishnets cut to be thigh highs that lift the butt, some sort of body harness, taping my labia to prevent any slipping, applying my pasties inexpertly (as I'd not needed them prior to that), cutting strips of the large roll of carpet tape I'd bought for the purpose, making sure my stage makeup was just so in less-than-perfect light, that my outer layer, the parts I was peeling, laid just right.

I was ready early so I got to see Kisa's whole act. Contrary to my assumption that this would not be a heavily attended event, it turns out convention goers love burlesque karaoke. The room was packed with a few hundred eager patrons. It was standing room only at the back and in the crowded doorways. The karaoke singer was in one corner of the stage. When the music began, Kisa ascended the stairs with studied disinterest, appearing to notice the audience only when they began to catcall and cheer for them.

They rolled their eyes. In one hand was a bag of Doritos, in the other a huge Slurpee. For the entire song Kisa toyed with the audience, not stripping at all, simply eating Doritos, giving them looks of contempt, striking poses in a skintight onesie, and then unceremoniously taking big noisy gulps of the Slurpee.

They took their time, crunching slowly, making eye contact with audience members. The room was on fire with appreciation for how they were owning everyone with the simple gift of their presence. They never even stripped. They made everyone grateful for the mere opportunity to watch this magnificent creature eat Doritos and drink a Slurpee. It was a boss-ass-bitch move, and I was completely shook. This human owned the entire room unapologetically while literally giving them nothing but actual crumbs, and still they thanked them. When they left the stage, the room erupted into a standing ovation. I stepped aside to let them come down the stairs off the side of the stage, wide eyed and shaking in my shoes. Kisa is a lovely and kind person. They broke their persona for just a moment to give me an encouraging grin and to tell me I was going to kill it. I'm sure I gave them a faltering nod in return, but inside I was a mess. I had to follow *that?*

I'd barely stripped for my husband before (doing striptease for an audience and being naked at a nude beach are very different things, after all), and now there were a few hundred people clamoring for me to take it all off to a song I might have never heard, and to do it without apology or reservation.

I swallowed, my mouth a desert. Oliver announced the next singer, and the person took the stage. I didn't know them, and I had no idea what was to come. I just knew I had been taking classes on burlesque movement for almost eighteen months. I knew I could move to a beat. I knew, intellectually, that I could do this, and probably do it well, or at least adequately, but could I meet *this* level of expectation right now? Lola had danced before Kisa, and while her performance had been more typical in terms of movement and striptease, it had been totally polished. You'd never have known that it wasn't a choreographed number. I knew that if I didn't push through it, I'd crumble under the certainty that I was going to disappoint a crowd that had been professionally primed.

And so the song was announced. I had no idea what it was, and the music started. I took slow, deliberate steps, climbing the stairs, trying to imbue my entire body with a take-no-prisoners attitude. I heard Roula in my head, telling me not to apologize for taking up space. I had turned my back to strike a pose, planning to coquettishly begin engaging the audience over my shoulder, when the music suddenly stopped. It was the wrong song. There was a technical glitch, rustling and hushed conversations from the table where Oliver was running things. The singer was off to the side of the stage, head down next to Oliver, looking at his screen, and I was alone.

Someone coughed. I heard people talking. Folks were getting up, and others were coming in. I did my best to become a stage prop, grateful beyond belief that my back was to the audience so they didn't have to see my lower lip trembling. I could feel my legs quaking to the same internal thrum, but I tried my best to keep them still. The moments dragged on for what felt like minutes but probably weren't. As my body quivered in anticipation, all the moments that had led to my being in that spot, in that space, in that time, washed over me.

I was a long way from the twentysomething woman who would never take her bra off in front of anyone out of embarrassment about how her breasts looked. I was miles from the thirtysomething woman who had lived in Spanx and sweated every inch of flesh that rolled under my clothing and "ruined" my silhouette despite the constricting and sweaty shapewear. I was a forty-five-year-old woman with fire-engine-red hair shaved on one side, full pouty glitter-red lips, and a plan to take off my clothes in front of a few hundred strangers (and some friends and my spouse) in the expectation that this would elicit delight and applause. I was a forty-five-year-old woman who was in the process of falling in love with myself and with my body, both the new shape of it and the old and stubborn jiggle and dimples of it too. I was a forty-five-year-old woman who was striving to stop apologizing for taking up space. I was ready, in fact, to take up all the space with all my magnificence. Because, damn it, I was, I am, magnificent. My body is juicy and warm and beautiful and fun and absurd. My skin had experienced the headiness of breathing the outdoor air and now, now I was going to show this huge room full of people that my body was and is worthy of all the things, not least of all their admiration and adulation. I slowed my breathing, closed my eyes, and when the music finally began in earnest, so did I.

Chapter Ten

BEING BONNIE

WHEN I HAD MY RECKONING AT AGE FORTY-TWO, the summer of my mother's death, I decided that before I turned fifty-five I was going to do everything I knew I wanted to do (plus say yes to all the things that remotely attracted me, even if they'd seemed outside the box I'd always lived in). At forty-two, thirteen years looked simultaneously ample and brief. I'm pleased to say that, with Dave's and our kids' support, I've made good use of the time. These are some of the things I've done in the past eight years:

+ Returned to a regular fitness practice. I'm not perfect with it, and I'm not making gains, but I'm holding steady and hopefully keeping the specter of brain death at bay.

+ Researched and undergone the breast reduction surgery I'd wanted since I was a teenager, as well as a tummy tuck to heal my split abdominal wall. I had LASIK surgery, freeing myself from contacts and glasses (other than now needing reading glasses at night). This was an incredible gift to myself, especially given the next item.

+ Recommitted myself to the passion of scuba diving, got recertified, and am now open water, advanced open water, and nitrox certified. I have eighty-five logged dives under my belt and am on track to complete dive one hundred in the next few months. This is excellent timing, because there's a tradition, for those courageous enough, to celebrate one's one-hundredth dive by doing it naked and . . .

+ Discovered the joy and freedom and release of social nudity, both before and after my surgeries, which has led to not only comfort in my own naked skin but actual celebration of my amazing body and all the pleasure it holds for me and for others.

+ Through a series of seemingly unconnected encounters, discovered the existence of burlesque as an art form, opening the doors for me to enter the fullness of my performative essence in the midst of middle age.

+ Reconnected with my own sexuality and lived it out loud. I claimed my queerness from the shadows and expanded my heart to embrace all the ways I am capable of loving.

+ Found my belonging spaces and nurtured them and the people and relationships in them. In so doing I've learned to fall in love with myself and to treat myself just as well as I treat the others I love.

+ Expanded my joy in giving, seeking opportunities to be a patron and a no-strings-attached supporter to artists and other creatives in need.

+ Recommitted to traveling for the joy of discovery and the depth of understanding that comes with each new place. I've added Belize, Guatemala, Roatán, Mexico, Grand Cayman (again), Jamaica, Saint Martin, the Bahamas, Indonesia, the Keys, Washington State, Oregon and Northern California (US 101 and the Pacific Coast Highway), and a return to South Africa to my list of places where I've connected with the earth and the ocean.

+ Celebrated my "fuck-it" forties with leaps of faith and rushes of adrenaline. I'm entering my fifties with intention and deliberate action to complete my list by fifty-five (which includes writing this book) and to relax my need to control every step, allowing more flow in my life and fostering more intimacy in all my relationships.

+ Continued practicing law as long as it served me and nourished my sense of self and service. When it came time to let it go, I did so, finding fulfillment in working with my husband at the business we own, learning a completely new set of work skills and cherishing all the challenges and growth and the certainty that we make a solid team in vocation and in adventure. I've also given myself freedom of time and purpose that was not possible when running a demanding solo practice family law firm.

+ Learned all the things I could about RV life after Covid upended our travel plans, engineered an opportunity to explore that world, and then bought a travel trailer and a truck to pull it, making it a monthly priority to explore the world we can reach within a long weekend.

+ Learned that unconditional love looks different than I thought. I've learned where my edges are, and where other people start and end. I've learned that I am responsible only for my own behavior and that I will not hold shame for others. I've learned that unconditional love means loving someone even though they aren't always who you want them to be. And I've learned that the gift of receiving that kind of love frees you up to love yourself and figure out exactly who you actually are once you no longer have to try to be the person you falsely believed you promised to be at the start. It also means accepting how unfinished we all are, being open to growth, even unexpected scary growth, and having the courage to be raw and real about that to the ones who matter most.

Chapter Eleven

TURNING YOUR SOMEDAYS & MAYBES INTO NOWS & HELL YESES!

OU'VE MADE IT THIS FAR, AND THAT TELLS ME THAT you're curious, and intrigued, maybe titillated by possibilities that hadn't occurred to you before. You are in pain. I know that, because pain is simply a feature of life. Pain of loss, pain of regret, pain of judgment, pain of shame, pain of fear.

You endure physical pain too. Pain born of stillness and pain born of exertion. Pain of carrying burdens and pain from bad things happening to good people. You, statistically speaking, probably have pain that you have learned to carry and which may always be with you in the form of diseases or conditions or syndromes or vestiges of old injury. I am not promising you control over every type of pain. The human body and mind is subject to so many random stressors and hurts that it would be an insult to you for me to suggest otherwise. But some pain is self-inflicted, and fluid.

Pain will always have a seat at your table, but that doesn't mean you have to invite every kind of pain to stay for dinner. Can you invite pain that offers growth and strength and flexibility into your life? Can you invite pain that challenges your fears and builds your sense of competence and confidence to the table? Can you send the pain that offers nothing but self-recrimination out of the room, even out of your house entirely? I can say with confidence that I now run my own guest list. The pains that I cannot banish get a lot quieter when I fill my table and my heart with the pain of vulnerability and courage. I don't believe that I'm magic in deciding who sits at my table, whom I choose to feed. You, too, can set your guest list and therefore the tone of the entire table. Take your seat at the head and don't hesitate one moment more.

When I meet new people, or open myself up to people who knew me already but only knew a curated side of me, or an older version of me, there is often surprise, and sometimes a bit of shock, and maybe a bit of judgment about the paths I've danced upon. I'm choosy about the people I allow in. I'm grateful that people who aren't willing to question and examine that judgment and explore what's on the other side of it are largely absent in my life. I don't get upset if someone has an initial negative reaction to behavior they may see as wild, immoral, or unbefitting my age or station in our world, but I do expect an openness to dialogue and a willingness to hear my story with an open heart if they want to stay in my life.

Still, variations of "How does your husband feel about this?"

and "Does your husband know about this?" are common questions. I have heard "And your husband *lets* you do this?" only a few times, thankfully.

My husband, Dave, had absolutely no idea what was in store when we met online in 2008 through Chemistry.com. I worked at a large insurance defense law firm in Atlanta. There I had a legal secretary, a hefty salary, and a closet full of business attire. He had no idea that I'd someday want to spend a week each year at a clothing-optional resort, or that I'd relish stripping and performing on stages around the city—and sometimes beyond—while strangers hoot and holler and throw money at me. He had no idea I'd push him to get scuba certified or that I'd take him skydiving or convince him to go to a Burning Man event.

He couldn't have known what would happen to my mother, or how the gift she gave me would change both of our lives, forever. Dave has a huge personality, a big presence despite his compact stature. He's frequently the loudest person in a gathering, and he interacts with the world and everyone in it with an exuberance that is charming and at times childlike. He had heard from women throughout his life that he needed to "tone it down" and "chill out." Just as Dave accepted me and loved me exactly where I was when we met, I did the same for him. His confidence, at times brashness, and the resonance of his voice in small spaces startled me quite a bit at first, but I recognized that to ask him to make himself smaller was to tell him that he wasn't lovable as he was. We fell for each other hard and fast, and we've always done our absolute best to love all of each other, not just the palatable facets of our personalities and habits.

So yes, my husband *does* support what I do. He's been my stable

base of exploration from the start of this journey. He's made countless sacrifices of time and comfort to facilitate me being the most
me that I can be. I only hope he feels as supported by me as I do
by him, although in truth I can't imagine I quite reach the bar he's
set. It's probably a good thing there aren't two performers in the
household (although he really *can* dance, and I'd love to get him on
stage someday).

He loves me unconditionally, and the way he has loved me these
past fifteen years has facilitated my journey to love myself. A good
marriage must be tended, but I'm grateful that with this man, it
very rarely feels like hard work, and when it is hard, it's also always
ultimately rewarding when we navigate the thing, whatever it was,
and find our way back to joyful connection.

Still, I live in a larger context than just my marriage. What about
the rest of my family? What about my children? What about their
friends and their parents? Our neighbors? Professional colleagues
and employees?

As far as burlesque goes, our kids have known about burlesque
since I began. There were about eighteen months between when I
first took a class and when I first stripped on stage, so by the time
I transitioned to doing solo striptease performances, they were no
longer fazed by it. They were also all teenagers by then, and I actually
relished the opportunity to be open with them about my journey to
reconnect with and let go of shame around my body.

The kids have never seen me striptease, but they have seen me
perform in group numbers with my troupe in festival settings (Atlanta
Pride), and they tell me they are proud of me (and apparently their
friends think I'm pretty much the coolest, so that's been fun). My

wives-in-law, as I'm fond of calling them (Dave's former wife and Clint's current wife) have also been supportive, and it has never impacted our coparenting with them. I know I'm incredibly lucky (I was a divorce and custody attorney, so I don't take any of my coparenting team for granted, ever).

My parental units (with my mother gone that includes my step-dad, Eric; my father, Dan; my former stepmother, Suzanne; and my dad's current wife, Judy) have all accepted me and supported me (and Dave) as well. Some more enthusiastically than others, but I know they love me even when we disagree, and we've negotiated the necessary boundaries to keep everyone comfortable with how close or far they want to be from Bonnie. Suzanne actually loves coming to shows, and I know that my mother would have too. That has been one of the great sadnesses of this part of my life. My mom was an incredible stage mom when I was in high school. She made costumes and helped with every facet of every dance recital, play, and football halftime show when I was in the flag corps and drill team. Whether it was tie-dyeing flags for us to twirl or hosting rehearsal parties in our basement, she always held my dreams and aspirations front and center.

I hate that she never got to go to a burlesque show, even without me in it. She fought with herself her entire life about her weight and her body, and she was never, to my awareness, comfortable in her own skin. I so wish she could have been here for the body-positivity movement, to see fat women own their sexual power without restraint on stages at all levels, from dive bars in Atlanta to the Grammy Awards. I wish she could have been here to talk to me about why I love going to clothing-optional resorts. I have no doubt she'd have amassed an enormous stockpile of rhinestones and that my costume wardrobe would be that much more sparkly if she were here than it is without her.

What about outside my family, though? Well, that was a bit more challenging. I began doing burlesque when we still had two kids in high school, both in marching band, and I was an enthusiastic band mom. I went to band camp each summer for four years in a row as part of a team of thirty parent chaperones with almost three hundred marching band members. High school is hard enough without being teased by your friends or classmates because one of your parents is doing burlesque. There were some great band parents in the group, but I knew that my extracurricular activities would make some parents believe I was an unfit influence, so for my first few years I maintained strict boundaries between my regular life (Shannon) and my sparkle life (Bonnie). I never mentioned burlesque in Shannon's social media, and I avoided talking about it around other parents.

There were a few who knew, who were close enough friends for me to trust, but it wasn't until our youngest finished his senior year marching band season that I became more open in that arena. I'm happy to say that I'm still friends with some of those band moms, and a few have even made it out to a show or two.

I was also still a lawyer when I began burlesque, and in that world I tried to maintain a really tall wall between Shannon and Bonnie. My practice was already part time by then, and I was focused on doing guardian ad litem (GAL) work. GALs are attorneys appointed by the court to represent the best interests of children in contested custody cases. In many juvenile court settings where cases of deprivation are being heard, GALs may be employed by the court itself, but in civil divorce and custody and visitation matters, GALs were simply attorneys appointed, typically at the request of one or both parties, to step into the case.

As a GAL, my fees were usually split by the parties, although the judge had the option to reapportion how my fees were paid at any point. My role as a GAL was different from that as a litigator. It was my job to do an investigation on the court's behalf and then make a recommendation to the judge on custody and parenting time that would serve the child's best interests. If the case went to trial, I had to prepare a written report, and I would participate as both an advocate for the child's best interests (meaning I remained in the courtroom for the entire trial and could, at the judge's discretion, cross-examine witnesses brought by either side), and as an expert witness.

In that capacity I typically spent several hours on the witness stand, explaining my recommendation and being cross-examined by the party who felt my recommendation went against their own interests. Certainly my doing burlesque had absolutely no relevance to my competence as a GAL or to any recommendation I ever made in any case in which I was appointed. But, as with the politics of being a band mom, I was clear eyed about the fact that I was a woman in a Southern state, appearing in courts that were at times outside the metro Atlanta area, in places where some judges still had a reputation for scolding women attorneys who had the audacity to wear pantsuits in their courtroom. In this context, my being a burlesque performer could undermine my credibility. Even if it weren't revealed in the courtroom, that sort of information could make a parent with whom I might be working to build rapport or to encourage into a settlement to not trust me, or even to think I shouldn't be allowed access to their children.

A few years into Bonnie's rise as a regular performer in the Atlanta burlesque scene, I was working a particularly difficult case in an outlying county. During an unannounced home visit at the father's house, just as I was about to leave, the father used my stage name. "So tell me more about Bonnie Bodacious. I'd love to come to a show sometime."

I froze. Because of what I had learned about this particular parent at that point, I knew that, despite his grin and his attempts to tell me how cool he thought it all was, it was possibly a veiled threat. I also knew that he had no social media presence himself, as he had claimed that he didn't trust "any of that stuff." He had a criminal history, and there were allegations of violence in the case at hand.

I played it off as casually as I could, trying to ascertain where he'd gotten the information, but he kept it vague, said a friend of a friend had come across it. His message seemed clear. I needed to make a recommendation in his favor or face exposure. I extricated myself, letting him know that he should not come to a show, as it wouldn't be appropriate, but doing my best to act like this was an entirely normal conversation.

Dave was waiting for me in the car. I told him to drive while I just breathed for a few miles. I knew what I had to do, and in hindsight I'm grateful that this thing I had feared finally happened. Keeping Bonnie and Shannon entirely separate was exhausting.

What was the worst thing that could come of this parent of my child client knowing about Bonnie? The worst would be that he didn't like the outcome of the case, blamed me, and sought violent retribution. That was a risk that every family lawyer lives with in every case, though, and that risk was already there before he knew about Bonnie. So the real risk was his exposing me to the attorneys and the judge. But even there, no matter how salacious the information, there really wasn't any relevance. The child whose interests I was representing was very young, so there couldn't be any argument that I was influencing them to grow up to be a stripper (which would, of course, have been a ridiculous assumption, no matter their age). If it were brought up to the judge, I did not see a way that it could be explicitly used to undermine my recommendation. But, if it caused a visceral reaction in the judge, then it could contribute to a bias against me and my recommendation. But more troubling than that was the threat it posed to my reputation and respect for my integrity.

The visit had happened on a Sunday afternoon. I got up the next morning and left voice mails for the attorneys representing the parents. I let them know that I needed to schedule a conference call with both of them as soon as possible, preferably that day. That afternoon, with both of them on the call, I told them about my burlesque life. The two attorneys, who were both taking extremely adversarial positions in the case on behalf of their clients, and who constantly complained about each other, were nonetheless both decent men and good attorneys. While they were definitely surprised, they agreed with me that my hobby was completely irrelevant to the case. I let them know that I needed to be up front about it, since the father had found Bonnie online, because no matter what happened, my sharing my truth with them took the power away from the father and removed any suggestion that his having that knowledge could impact my recommendation.

Both attorneys agreed and, most importantly, the father's attorney assured me he would not attempt to use the information with the court to gain an advantage. While I appreciated that assurance, and I trusted it was made in good faith, I also know what it's like to be pressured by an unhappy client in the midst of a volatile trial.

After the final hearing was scheduled, I took some time after my normal trial preparations for a contested custody trial and prepared to respond to Bonnie being revealed to the world in open court. In the interim months I had gone to every performance with Dave at my back, keeping an eye out for the father, or more likely one of his "associates," in case he decided to press the intimidation factor. I didn't think, pretrial, that he'd actually commit an act of violence, but I figured he might want photo or video evidence, since I'd taken away the power he thought he had in the mere knowledge that Bonnie existed. It was a tense few months, but I refused to stop being Bonnie. I refused to be terrorized into smallness.

As I sat on the witness stand off and on for hours during the incredibly contentious trial, defending my recommendation that the mother have custody, I watched the father get more and more frustrated and animated in his whispered conversations with his attorney. I felt grounded and ready to explain who Bonnie was, who I was, without apology or shame, even if they pulled out a giant photo of me frolicking nearly naked on a stage with dollar bills flying through the air. In that moment, I had no more fear. In that moment, I knew viscerally what I'd already known cerebrally: I am Bonnie. I am Shannon. And it was time to stop donning any vestiges of shame every time I stepped out of Bonnie and into Shannon.

The attorney kept his word. Bonnie was not revealed in court, but it didn't matter. Ultimately word got around. I stopped being so careful after that case. I started being more open with my lawyer friends. I realized that being the source of the story was a much more powerful position, and I never wanted to feel on the defensive about how I choose to take up space again. And, despite it all, there were still attorneys asking for me to be appointed, and still judges who wanted to appoint me. I'm grateful for my career as a lawyer, for all I learned and all I offered. I have some great war stories. I am proud of the real good that I did in people's lives, and I'm also content that it's over. I'm ready to find all the new ways I can grow and learn for the time I have left in this world with my brain intact.

So, in the end, if you find yourself saying, *I can't pursue this dream or that adventure, because what about . . . ?* Lean into that question. Examine it from all angles. It is reasonable to make concessions for convention where your safety and access to basic human needs are involved. It is reasonable to make concessions to convention to protect those who depend upon you. But it is also reasonable to question the realities we've always accepted. I know that I am privileged in that the worst consequence of my coming out of the cocoon has been occasional discomfort (mine and others) and moments of fear, hard conversations, and reconciliations. But I didn't know that those would be the worst consequences. I had to trust first and foremost that I had the tools within me to navigate the uncharted paths. I had to trust that my drive to avoid the regret that caused such anguish for my mother in her last years of lucidity was valid and worth following. I had to trust that it was not my job to ensure the comfort of everyone around me. It is not your job to accept future regret to protect others from present discomfort.

I'm not done, not close to being done. I've got less than five years till my hopefully arbitrary and not-prescient deadline of fifty-five, and I have a lot more life to live. More travel. More adventure. More love. More writing. More performing with vulnerability and power. More inspiring others to find their way back to their own bodies and selves. I am becoming a touchstone for humans trying to find their way to fall in love with themselves, to stop apologizing for taking up space, to start luxuriating in their own magnificence and even sharing it should they so choose. Let me hear from you, dear reader. Let's talk, because this conversation is only the beginning.

I live out loud. The people who matter are still with me. The people who don't saw themselves out. And I'm ready to continue to relish pleasure and joy—in my body, in connection with others, in connection with the earth, for as many years as I have left with a functioning brain and body. Everything that happens from here on out is sweet, sweet gravy.

Join me, nourish your heart and your flesh, your curiosity and your creativity. You are not too old, too fat, too soft, too calloused, too thin, too damaged, too lost. You owe yourself no apologies. You've read this book, which I hope has shown you at the very least how kind you can be to yourself. Follow your eager and curious heart when it tugs. You are the only one who can feel and honor where it is called. You deserve no less than sweet, sweet gravy of your own.

ᴬDMISSIBLE ᴱVIDENCE

Want to see the admissible evidence of this journey?

Go to bonniebodacious.com/gallery (or scan the QR code) to see the evidentiary files!

ACKNOWLEDGMENTS

First and foremost, I acknowledge the unconditional support of my spouse, Dave Hinkleman, who has loved me unabashedly, and unwaveringly through every iteration of myself as my own greatest art project. He threw himself into loving me and our family like it was his foundational purpose. No matter which brambly, unlit, frightening path I suddenly started running down next, he took stock of what he needed to keep us safe, and then followed me unflinchingly, never questioning whether I knew where the hell I was going (I mostly did not). This was a hell of a year for me to insist this book needed to happen, and he rolled with it as he always does, with impeccable grace and style.

I also acknowledge the love and support of our children: Max, Rae (formerly known as Abby), and Chase. We threw some curve-balls at you over the years, and I'm grateful that you've become such incredibly kind and emotionally intelligent young adults. *The kids really are alright ya'll!*

I also acknowledge and thank our extended parenting family: Clint, Irene, and Liz. I know what most divorced and blended family constellations look like and I'm incredibly honored and inspired by the ways we've walked this path together. Knowing that I'm part of a team has always made it more possible for me to pursue my own passions and that is a privilege that I acknowledge with gratitude.

To my family of origin: my dad and his wife Judy, my second mom Suzanne, my Aunt Lauren, my bonus dad Eric, and my Aunt Terry, thank you for coming along for this ride that is my life, and being there for me when I've stumbled and when I've summited.

To the people who sweated and cried with me through the moments of real growth, my Operation Boot Camp family (Heidi, Jeff, JoJo, Tim, Shaunya, and Chester) and my long suffering and incredibly patient personal trainer, Jason.

And of course, to the mentors and teachers and inspirers and backstage shenanigan masters, my sparkle family at Metropolitan Studios (Roula, Talloolah, Ursula, and Lola along with all my Candybox Revue Confections past and present) your gifts of time and energy to lift up our community are changing the world. You are all inspirations to me and I will always raise you up in every way I can!

And finally, to the book midwife and publishing guru team of Fen Druadin and Kory Kirby, this might have eventually happened without you, but it's hard for me to imagine how. Your patience and encouragement and presence in my life this past year have been transformative. THANK YOU for making sure I didn't die with the regret of not having completed this project.

ABOUT THE AUTHOR

A little bit wonk and a little bit wild, Shannon has roamed many paths over her fifty years. She's been a dancer, a survivor, an actress, a traveler, a therapist, a lawyer, a scuba diver, a photographer, a lover of clothing-optional resorts, and the badass burlesque performer Bonnie Bodacious. She was emboldened to say yes to her heart after her mother was diagnosed with early-onset dementia, highlighting the risk in Shannon's own genetic makeup. Confronted with the reality that life could be shorter than she thought, Shannon stopped living reactively and started saying yes to one adventure after another. From carrying the weight of self-loathing in her twenties to living out loud naked (or nearly naked) without apology in middle age, Shannon now embraces unabashed self-love and celebration. She lives in Atlanta with her husband and dogs.

bonnie@bonniebodacious.com
bonniebodacious.com

If you enjoyed this book, please head to Amazon and leave an honest review. Reviews help in my mission to inspire and empower people to claim themselves and live out loud! Thank you for your support. ♥

www.ingramcontent.com/pod-product-compliance
Lightning Source LLC
Chambersburg PA
CBHW030302130626
46549CB00002B/650